AF335342

THE MISSIONARY HEROES
OF AFRICA

J. H. MORRISON, M.A.

THE MISSIONARY HEROES OF AFRICA

BY

J. H. MORRISON, M.A.

NEGRO UNIVERSITIES PRESS

NEW YORK

Originally published in 1922
by George H. Doran Co., New York

Reprinted 1969 by
Negro Universities Press
A Division of Greenwood Publishing Corp.
New York

SBN 8371-1738-0

PREFACE

It is no easy task to determine what names should stand in the front rank of the Missionary Heroes of Africa. In making his selection the present writer has at least the consolation of believing that while many, doubtless, would desire some honored name to be added, few would wish any name on the list to be displaced.

The following sketches are offered in the hope that, brief and imperfect as they are, they may serve to communicate some spark of that divine fire which burns in all heroic lives, and nowhere clearer than in the lives of Christlike and Apostolic men. In the hope, also, that they may aid the imagination in forming some picture of the marvelously varied and romantic scenery of the African mission field.

CONTENTS

PAGE

CONTENTS

THE MISSIONARY HEROES OF AFRICA

MAP OF AFRICA

Showing the missionary stations where these heroes of African missions labored.

THE MISSIONARY HEROES OF AFRICA

CHAPTER I

THE DARK CONTINENT BEFORE THE DAWN

All Gaul, as Cæsar says, is divided into three parts. All Africa may be divided into two. These are the Northern and the Southern halves of the continent, which are found to differ widely both in history and in religion.

I: *Mohammedan Africa*

From the earliest times North Africa played a conspicuous part in the ancient world which centred round the Mediterranean. The names of Egypt and Carthage are a sufficient reminder to us of that. Accordingly it was among the first countries to be evangelised, and in the early Christian centuries the vigorous Churches of North Africa produced men like Augustine and Tertullian, Clement and Origen. Of these ancient churches only a wretched remnant survives in Abyssinia.

In the seventh century the tide of Islam, which flowed north over the churches of Asia, flowed also westward and swept away the Christianity of North Africa. Since then the Mohammedan faith has more than maintained its ground in Africa. It has gradually spread southward, down the east coast to Zanzibar, across the Sudan to the Niger and the Gulf of Guinea, until to-day it dominates half the continent. No doubt it is fitted to give to savage tribes a certain moral and religious uplift, but its cast iron system blocks all farther progress and makes its converts less accessible to the Gospel than before. In Mohammedan Africa Christian missions have made little progress to speak of, and our concern is therefore with pagan Africa which forms the central and southern half of the continent. It must not be forgotten, however, that Islam is still a living and missionary force, and part of the urgency of African evangelisation lies in this, that if the advance of the Cross be delayed the Crescent may take possession of the whole field.

II: *Pagan Africa*

In the 15th century bold voyagers had begun to venture down the west coast, and before the close of the century they had rounded the Cape of Good Hope. From this time forward an increasing volume of trade was carried on with Africa, and settlements were planted along the coasts, west, south and east. Nothing, however, was known as yet of the interior, which remained a blank on the map till the 19th century. It was vaguely conceived as a vast and inhospitable desert. Only through the travels of David Livingstone and other explorers were its natural features, its lakes and river systems, made known to the world. It was then discovered that the interior of Africa consists of a vast, undulating plateau, having a climate very different from that of the low, swampy coast-land, much of it very fertile, much of it suitable for European colonisation.

Pagan Africa is mainly inhabited by two races of coloured people, the Negroes and the Bantus. Besides these another race may be mentioned, though numerically insignificant, namely the Hottentots and Bushmen. These lived in the neighbourhood of Cape Town and the districts to the north, consequently they figure somewhat prominently in early colonial and missionary history. Probably they are a remnant of the aboriginal inhabitants of Africa who have been driven south by the incoming of stronger tribes. The Bushmen are almost if not quite extinct. They were pigmies with light coloured skin, and in their habits pure nomads. Wondering continually about, trapping game, carrying off cattle, and shooting man and beast with their poisoned arrows, they were regarded by colonists and natives alike, as vermin to be exterminated. Their kinsmen, the Hottentots, were more settled in their habits, and have gradually become intermingled with other tribes. It is undoubtedly from the Bushmen and Hottentot language that certain of the southern Bantu tribes have borrowed those curious little explosives in speech, common known as "Kafir clicks."

Of the two great races, the Negroes inhabit the north of Central Africa from the Sahara to nearly the Equator, and from the Nile valley westward to the Gulf of Guinea and the regions of the Niger. To this race belong such numerous and powerful peoples as the Sudanese, the Hausas, etc. The Bantu race, greatest of all the African peoples, occupies practically the whole of South Africa up to the Equator and five degrees beyond it. It includes among its tribes all the names most familiar in South African history— Kafir, Zulu, Matabele, Basuto, Bechuana. North of the Zambesi it embraces all the peoples from Barotsiland to Uganda. Its three hundred languages and dialects have a close affinity, being all built on what is called a syntax of euphony, according to which the sound of the ruling word pervades the sentence. Roughly it is as if in English, instead of saying, "Men (women, children) go to church," we should say, "Men me-go me-church, Women we-go we-church, Children chi-go chi-church." The Bantu tribes were comparatively late arrivals in Africa and their warlike migrations lasted till well on in the nineteenth century. In colour they are dark brown rather than black, and many have sharp, finely chiselled features. In this connection it may be remarked that the variety of features and of facial expression among Africans generally, both Negro and Bantu, is as great as among Europeans. The typical representation of the negro face is as much a caricature as the portly John Bull or the lanky Uncle Sam.

The religion of pagan Africa takes the form of Fetichism, which is rather a system of vague and gloomy superstitions than a body of definite religious beliefs. The African feels himself to be surrounded by a world of spirits, malignant and terrifying. These spirits may reside in any object, animate or inanimate, they may enter and take possession of a human being. They have practically an unlimited power of working deadly mischief on every hand. The African is like a superstitious man walking along a dark road, who feels that a sheeted ghost may start from every bush, and knows not at what moment he may find himself in the grip of clammy hands. It is not to be wondered at that men in this condition are driven crazy with fear, swept away at times with wild panic, and ready to purchase safety by the most dreadful rites and sacrifices.

Hence arises the power of the witch doctor. He alone has knowledge of the spirit world. He alone can "smell out" the spirits, can appease them or drive them off. His commands, however terrible, must be obeyed. There is no help for it, unless one is prepared to deliver one's self over to still more awful, because invisible, terrors. Doubtless the witch doctors have been more or less sincere in their self-delusions, but they have often abused their dread powers for private ends, of self interest or of revenge. Suspected persons were made to undergo an ordeal by poison, those who survived being accounted innocent, those who died, guilty. This ordeal was applied not merely to single individuals but sometimes to whole villages at once. How terrific the power of the witch doctor was may be gathered from the fact that in 1856 the Kafirs were persuaded to destroy all their cattle, thus reducing themselves to abject starvation, in the hope that on a certain day countless herds would rise from the dead, and usher in an African millenium.

In some parts of Africa cannibalism was practised,

though not to any great extent. Infanticide was more widely prevalent, and twins especially, being regarded by some tribes as monstrosities, were cast out to die. Cruel and bloody funeral rites often followed the death of a chief. In order that his spirit might be suitably attended in the underworld, numbers of his slaves were put to death. In some cases his wives were buried alive in the grave with him.

Repulsive as these rites and practices of paganism are,—so repulsive that the worst cannot be told—yet it will invariably be found that they are not the product of sheer, wanton deviltry, but that there is some serious thought, however blinded, underlying them, and some serious intention, however gross, prompting them. It would also be a grave mistake to picture the moral and social life of the African as a condition of unrelieved darkness. There are laws of friendship and hospitality, standards of decency and respectability, which are as strictly observed as among other nations, the wisdom of the fathers, such as it is,— and some of it is not contemptible—is carefully passed on to the children, and there is always to be found some degree of that natural affection and humanity without which social life would be impossible.

Yet when every allowance is made it is a dark and pitiful picture that remains. A false idea of God distorts all human thought and shrouds this mortal life in universal gloom. Instead of a kindly Providence above there is the haunting presence of devils; instead of a divine, redeeming love there is a devilish anger to be appeased and devilish cruelty to be satisfied with blood; instead of a Heavenly Father to whom His children can look with confidence for help, there are spirit forces embattled round a man, against whose demonic energy he must pit his puny strength, and from whom he can hope to wring a gift only by paying some terrible price. "Paganism," writes Dr. Stewart, "is a terrible fate spiritually, and an oppressive power under which to live. To all the ills of life it adds the constant terrors of a world unseen, whose agents are ever actively interfering with human affairs, and from which there is no escape. . . . The darkest picture is not overdrawn. The poorness and hardness, narrowness and joylessness of human existence in paganism, in Central Africa at least, must be seen to be understood." More than 100 millions of the people of Africa live under this blight.

Opponents of missions have at times amused themselves with fanciful pictures of the natural state of the heathen world, a state of sweet innocence and peace, which it were cruelty to disturb. No such state ever existed in Africa. Even before the incoming of the white race Africa was continually the scene of bloody wars and revolutions. The tribal chief was often a cruel, bloodthirsty and licentious tyrant who ate up his people. Neighbouring tribes, instead of living peacefully side by side, were usually at war. From time to time vast convulsions took place, when some barbarous tribe suddenly burst into activity like a volcano, and spread ruin far and wide. The Zulus are a notable instance of this. About the beginning of the nineteenth century they were ruled by a great chief, Chaka, who has not unfitly been called the Napoleon of South Africa. He welded his warriors together by an iron military discipline, and sent out army after army to plunder and devastate. It has been estimated that at least a million human beings were thus wantonly exterminated. Even the flying splinters of Chaka's armies were formidable. Of these the best known are the Matabele who laid waste Southern Rhodesia, the Mantiti who, after threatening Cape Colony, streamed away to the northwest and conquered the tribes of the upper Zambesi, and the Angoni who became the terror of Nyasaland. Such was heathen life in Africa.

III: *The Hand of Europe*

It cannot be denied, however, that contact with Europe brought upon Africa new and vast evils. Of these the greatest and most indefensible was the slave trade. It began shortly after the discovery of America. The miserable Indians were being rapidly exterminated under the tyranny of Spain, and the demand for labour became more pressing. In these circumstances the west coast of Africa became the recruiting ground for the plantations of the New World. The traffic from the first was, confessedly, an outrage on humanity, but so enormously profitable did it prove to be that all religious scruples and moral considerations were swept aside. Portugal and Spain led the way, but soon England outstripped them, and at one time she had nearly 200 vessels engaged exclusively in the trade. One company alone was chartered to supply 30,000 slaves annually to the West Indies. In this way millions of the people of Africa were transported across the Atlantic and millions more were cruelly done to death. The slavetraders harried the west coast from Cape Verde and round the Gulf of Guinea to the Congo. They burned villages and kidnapped the inhabitants, they encouraged intertribal wars and bought the prisoners, they planted trading stations along the coast where guns and gin were exchanged for human beings, they organised slave hunting in the interior. Meantime a similar stream of Africa's lifeblood was pouring out through the gates of the east coast to supply the slave markets of Asia. This continued long after the Trans-Atlantic traffic was suppressed. Indeed the stream, though now greatly diminished, has not yet entirely ceased to flow. In Livingstone's day it was running full flood. Populous regions round Lake Nyasa were being devastated, the forest paths leading to the coast were filled with strings of fettered captives, and along the line of march were strewn the skeletons of those who had fallen. Gradually the conscience of Christendom awoke, and the nineteenth century saw the practical extinction of this inhuman traffic.

The history of European colonisation in Africa runs back over four hundred years. By the sixteenth century the Portuguese were firmly settled on both the east and west coasts. The old grey castle of Mozambique was built by Albuquerque in 1508, and St. Paul de Loanda was founded seventy years later. These tropical regions, however, can never become a white man's country, and the Portuguese settlements have too often shown a sad record of physical and moral degeneration. Yet Portugal has conferred important benefits on Africa by the introduction into the country of various new articles of food, such as oranges and lemons, maize and sweet potatoes, and many other vegetables. As has been said, "Take away from the African's food all that the Portuguese have introduced and he would be left very poorly supplied with the necessaries of life."

The real colonisation of Africa began at Cape Town and proceeded northwards. In the reign of James I, two British admirals, Shillinge and Fitz Herbert, landed at the Cape and, with an amazing imperial and prophetic spirit, took possession in the name of Britain of "the South African coast and continent!" Their action, however, was not followed up, and in 1652 Holland stepped in and held the Cape for a century and a half. At the close of the Napoleonic wars it fell to Britain and the tide of colonisation set steadily in. The conflicts between Dutch and British interests, which lasted throughout the nineteenth century, promoted expansion northward, and now Dutch and British are happily joined in the United States of South Africa.

It was not till the last quarter of the nineteenth century that the scramble for Africa began. The discoveries of Livingstone and other travellers had revealed the enormous resources of the interior, industrial Europe was in want of raw material for her industries, and of new markets for her finished products. Africa promised to supply both. Therefore Africa was divided up as spoil for the strong. Some of the results of this partition make painful reading, especially the atrocities of the Congo Free State. Free

State, indeed!—a vast region of tropical Africa placed at the mercy of a licentious king and a greedy group of financiers in Belgium, who glutted themselves with red rubber,—red with the lifeblood of the unhappy wretches by whose labours and tortures it was produced. Fortunately this has been the exception, and it cannot be doubted that the partition of Africa and its control by the nations of Europe has proved on the whole a blessing to the African. It has led to the abolition of many cruel rites, it has restrained intertribal war, it has protected the African to some extent from the aggressions of lawless white men, and given him, often for the first time, the blessings of good government and settled peace.

IV: *The Coming of the Missionary*

The colonisation of Africa has been accompanied, and in many cases preceded, by Christian missionary effort. Prince Henry of Portugal, who sent out the first bold voyagers to feel their way round the continent, was animated by a noble desire to promote the spread of the Christian faith, and stem the flowing tide of Islam. "Plant the Cross on some new headland. That is what I want," he said. As early as 1491 Dominican missionaries made an imposing start on the Congo, and for a time their labours were rewarded with great outward success. No real impression, however, was made upon the ignorance and barbarism of the people, and that, together with the unworthy lives of the missionaries, brought all to ruin. The Jesuits also laboured with zeal and devotion in all the Portuguese colonies, and penetrated some distance into the interior, but their work, like that of the Dominicans, had no solid basis of Christian education, and when they were banished from the colonies for political reasons, it fell to pieces. Only a few ruined walls remain to witness to the work which the mediæval Church attempted to do for Africa. It may be that some dim impressions of that work still linger in the African mind. Some years ago a remote heathen tribe on the Zambesi was found to possess a melody which proved to be a pure bit of fifteenth century church music, a melody moreover which had disappeared from the Portuguese churches about the end of the sixteenth century. This may well suggest the interesting question whether some of those African traditions which bear a resemblance to Scripture may not be derived from the same source.

In the eighteenth century Protestant missions entered the field, the Moravians as usual leading the way. They were followed by the London Missionary Society, the Church Missionary Society and others. It was not till the nineteenth century, however, that much progress was made, and the work established on a firm and enduring basis. Then began that wide-spread and hopeful process of Christian education and training which has done so much for the transformation of Africa and the uplift of its people. Then appeared a succession of missionary heroes, whose courage and endurance, whose devotion and holy zeal have been an inspiration to the Christian world, and whose names will ever be held in remembrance as the founders of the African Church.

It should never be forgotten, however, that to African eyes these things wear a different aspect. The vast convulsions, the overthrow of the old order of things, the inferior position of the natives under the white man's rule, may well appear to them to be but doubtful blessings. When Mary Slessor was about to sail for Calabar she stood on deck and watched the boat being loaded with casks of spirits for the West Coast trade. "Scores of casks," she exclaimed sorrowfully, "and only one missionary." It was a sharp reminder of what is often forgotten in church circles, that Christian mission work is but one small element in the manifold activities of the white man. The missionary preaches brotherhood, but the colonist refuses to give the right hand of fellowship to his black brother. The pure influence of the Gospel is countered by the corruptions of city life. It need not, therefore, be surprising if many Africans, ignorant of the darkness and barbarism of the past, are impatient under the restraints and disabilities of their present condition, if some are bitterly resentful, and would fiercely deny that the white man's coming has brought the dawn. Yet, surely, the dawn it is, dubious and stormy, doubtless, at its first appearing, and with much darkness mingling with its light, but destined, by the blessing of God and the efforts of His people, to usher in for Africa a brighter day.

CHAPTER II

ROBERT MOFFAT, MISSIONARY PIONEER

I: *A Scots Gardener*

Robert Moffat was born at Ormiston in East Lothian on December 21, 1795. His boyhood, however, was spent at Portsoy on the Moray Firth and at Carronshore near Falkirk. When fourteen years old he was apprenticed as a gardener and for some time lived in a bothy with seven other men, not altogether a bad preparation for the rough life of a pioneer missionary. He grew up, a tall, strong lad, with dark, piercing eyes and a frame capable of more than ordinary endurance. He became a powerful swimmer, and on one occasion rescued a companion from drowning in the Firth of Forth. On finishing his apprenticeship he obtained a situation at High Leigh in Cheshire where he came into contact with the Methodists, to whom he owed his conversion. From childhood he had been under strong Christian influences. Both his parents were deeply religious after the somewhat stern old Scottish type of piety, and his mother had exacted from him, on leaving home, a solemn promise to read his Bible every day. Now, however, they were not without some suspicion of the confident faith and warm religious feeling that breathed through their son's letters. His father, while welcoming the news of his conversion "as cold water to a thirsty soul," proceeded at some length to exhort his son "not to be high-minded but to fear," and to this he added the warning, "Let him that thinketh he standeth take heed lest he fall."

Mainly through the influence of Mr. Roby of Manchester, Moffat's mind now began to turn to the mission field. The seed had indeed been sown much earlier in his childhood's home. Writing to his aged mother after many years of service in Africa Moffat warmly acknowledges this. "Mother, dear mother, your many prayers have been heard. . . . Wherever I am I never forget how much I owe to your prayers. The first dawn of reflection respecting my soul commenced with hearing you pray." His mother's influence seems to have been felt in other ways. "My dear old mother, to keep us out of mischief in the long winter evenings, taught me both to sew and knit, and when I told her I intended being a man, she would reply, 'Lad, ye dinna ken whaur your lot will be cast.'" While the circle round the fire was thus usefully employed their mother was accustomed to read such missionary news as was then to be had, especially the heroic stories of the labours and sufferings of the Moravians in Greenland and among the plantation slaves in the East Indies. Now it became the settled ambition of young Moffat to emulate these pioneers of the Gospel among the heathen.

Mr. Roby, in order to have his young friend nearer him for supervision and help, got work for him in the nursery garden of Mr. Smith of Dukinfield, a warm supporter of missions. "Thus was I led by a way that I knew not," writes Moffat, "for another important end, for otherwise I might not have had my late dear wife to be my companion and partner in all my hopes and fears for more than half a century in Africa. As it was, Mr. Smith's only daughter possessing a warm missionary heart, we soon became attached to one another, but she was not allowed to join me in Africa till nearly three years after I left." In physique the future Mrs. Moffat presented a contrast to her husband, being under ordinary height, with blue eyes, and a complexion that never lost its delicate girlish bloom. She was never strong and often her mind was oppressed by gloomy forebodings, but so perfectly did she become united with her husband in mutual love and trust, and in all their religious aspirations and labours, that their life story was fittingly recorded by their son in one common biography, *The Lives of Robert and Mary Moffat.*

After a first application to the London Missionary Society had been refused Moffat was at length, through the influence of his friend Mr. Roby, accepted for service in Africa. On September 30, 1816, he was solemnly set apart for the work, with eight others, at a meeting in Surrey Chapel, London. Five of the young missionaries were allocated to Africa, four to the South Seas. Among the latter was John Williams, the Apostle of Polynesia, whose devoted life was destined to be crowned by glorious martyrdom on Erromanga. It seemed at one moment as if Moffat and Williams would have more than a passing connection, for it was proposed that both should go to the South Seas. Dr. Waugh, however, a Scots member of the committee, protested that "thae twa lads are ower young to gang thegither." Thus the little turn was given that determined a great career.

II: *The Infant Colony*

Moffat and his companions reached Cape Town in January, 1817. The Colony was then in its infancy, for only three years had elapsed since British power was established as paramount at the Cape. Of vital importance as the half way house to India, it was first occupied by the Dutch, then seized by the French, and so continued a bone of contention throughout the period of the Napoleonic wars. The Colony now extended northward to the Orange River, but in reality its northern boundary was vague and undefined. Scarcely a sprinkling of white settlers was scattered over the vast area, while roving bands of Boers kept moving farther into the interior, hoping thus to leave British justice behind them, and enjoy unfettered liberty to enslave the native races. Crossing the Orange River they occupied the territory between the Orange and Vaal Rivers, then, having crossed the Vaal, they spread themselves thinly over the country to the north, up to the Limpopo. Thus were laid the foundations of what became the Orange Free State and the Transvaal, whose relations to British rule were to prove a source of ever recurring trouble for nearly a centuy, and whose determined hostility to Christian missions had much to do in determining the work of Moffat and the career of Livingstone.

The multitudinous tribes of natives, Bantu in the east and centre, Hottentot and Bushman in the west, were in a continual state of unrest. Intertribal wars and especially the wholesale devastations of the Zulu chief, Chaka, caused frequent migrations, with the inevitable accompaniment of bloodshed and plundering. In addition, the increasing pressure of white settlers who rode rough-shod over native rights led to a growing bitterness which ever and anon burst forth in savage outrage and equally savage reprisal. Accordingly, life along the northern border of the Colony was full of ever recurring perils and alarms.

North of the Orange River there stretches east and west a strip of barely habitable country called Great Namaqualand which becomes more parched and barren towards the north till it merges into the Kalahari Desert. Here was the home of various tribes of Hottentots and Bushmen, while the somewhat more fertile region to the east, bordering on the Transvaal, was inhabited by the Bechuanas, a Bantu tribe. Many of these Hottentots had retired over the Orange River to escape the advancing tide of civilization, and their land being beyond the Colony gradually became the refuge of native marauders and malcontents. Perhaps the most powerful element in the country was the Griquas or Bastards, a group of Hottentots with some infusion of Dutch blood, whose possession of firearms and of horses made them irresistible against a purely native force. Their principal settlement was at Griqua Town not far from the junction of the Orange River and the Vaal.

III: *Taming a Freebooter*

In Great Namaqualand the London Missionary Society had been at work before Moffat's arrival. The Bushmen were found almost impossible to evangelise, owing to their being pure nomads with neither homes nor settlements of any kind. Among the other Hottentots some slight progress had been made. In particular the chief, Africaner, who for years had been the terror of the border, was favourably impressed. It was to his kraal that Moffat was now directed to proceed. The Government of the Cape at first refused permission to travel beyond the frontier, evidently from some vague idea that missionary work would tend to consolidate the roaming tribes and freebooters, and make them more dangerous to the Colony. This caused a delay of several months, which Moffat spent at Stellenbosch in acquiring the Dutch language. The veto of the Government having been at length withdrawn, Moffat travelled north, crossed the Orange River and reached Africaner's kraal in January, 1818, a year after his landing at the Cape. A Mr. Ebner, who had been at work here for some time previously but who, through some disagreement with Africaner's people, felt his life to be in danger, immediately departed on Moffat's arrival, and the young missionary was left alone to make the best of his novel and difficult position.

Moffat's stay in Namaqualand did not extend to two years, yet his connection with Africaner and the influence he exerted over that once wild and lawless bandit is one of the most romantic episodes in his life.

On his journey north he had heard from Dutch farmers the most gloomy forebodings of the fate awaiting him. Some of their kindly *vrouws* even shed tears over this bonnie Scotch laddie going to an untimely death. Africaner was an outlaw upon whose head the Cape Government had set a price, and any hope that he might "tak' a thought and mend" was no more regarded than the ravings of lunacy.

Africaner's reception, though cool, was not unfriendly. By his order a rude hut was speedily erected in which Moffat settled down to a life of primitive simplicity. His meagre salary of £25 per annum was of no immediate use to him and he was compelled to subsist entirely on native food, chiefly milk and flesh. Often he had to tighten his belt over an empty stomach. The people among whom he laboured seemed hopelessly degraded. The constant struggle for a bare existence left no room for religion and but little for natural affection. The idea of God and the sense of right and wrong could hardly be said to exist. Undesirable infants were cast away and helpless old people left to perish.

In pleasing contrast was the earnestness of the chief, Africaner, who from the first seemed eager to learn and placed himself day by day with the utmost regularity under Moffat's teaching. He made rapid progress in Christian knowledge and character and actively promoted the work of the mission. The situation of his people, however, became impossible through long continued drought, and Africaner along with Moffat undertook a long journey to the north in the hope of finding a place suitable for a permanent settlement. In this they were unsuccessful, and returned after enduring many hardships in the desert. Moffat next went eastward to inspect a location offered to Africaner's people by the chiefs of the Griquas. On this journey he unwittingly drank of a pool which had been poisoned by the Bushman to kill game. Fortunately the effects passed off after a few days' illness. Having satisfied himself that Africaner should move east to Griqualand he returned and reported to the chief, who cordially agreed.

Moffat was now arranging to travel to Cape Town to meet his future wife, and to confer with deputies of the London Missionary Society who had been sent out to inquire into the work in South Africa. He proposed to Africaner to accompany him. At first the chief was startled and his people were thrown into violent alarm at the bare idea. For an outlaw, with a reward of £100 offered for his head, it might well seem madness to cross the Orange River, and the proposal was open to the suspicion of treachery. Moffat, however, saw great possibilities of good in reconciling the chief to the Government, and in exhibiting to friends and enemies of the mission this extraordinary trophy of the Gospel. Africaner at length consented and travelled through the Colony in disguise as Moffat's servant. On several occasions he had the curious experience of hearing Dutch farmers declare their utter scepticism as to his conversion, while they little dreamed that the subject of their remarks was standing by. Moffat himself was an object of interest. He tells with amusement of the alarm of one worthy farmer who took him for a ghost. "Everybody says you were murdered," he exclaimed, "and a man told me he had seen your bones." When informed that Africaner was now "a truly godly man," he replied, "I can believe almost anything you say but *that* I cannot credit. There are seven wonders in the world, that would be the eighth." At length, half convinced, he said, "Well, if what you say is true, I have only one wish and that is to see him before I die, and when you return, as sure as the sun is over our heads, I will go with you to see him, though he killed my own uncle." Trusting the discretion and goodwill of the farmer, Moffat said, "This is Africaner." The farmer was thunderstruck, but when by a few questions he had assured himself of the fact, he lifted up his eyes and exclaimed, "O God, what a miracle of Thy power! What cannot Thy grace accomplish?"

The Governor of the Cape, Lord Charles Somerset, was equally sceptical at first, but Moffat's assurances and still more the appearance and manners of Africaner convinced him of the reality of the miracle, and eventually the Government reward offered for the head of the freebooter was spent in buying him a wagon in which he safely returned home to his people.

Moffat now received instructions to proceed to Bechuanaland which lies to the east of the Kalahari Desert, between that region of desolation and the Transvaal. His destination was Kuruman, a hundred miles north of Griqua Town, but after crossing the Orange River he was detained for several months in Griqua Town, waiting Government permission to go north. Here he parted, for the last time as it proved, from his friend Africaner. The chief had

brought Moffat's goods across country from Namaqualand in his wagon, and he left hoping soon to bring
his people east to Griqualand, but this design was frustrated by his death.

Griqua Town was at this time peopled by a miscel-
laneous collection of Griquas, Hottentots and Bushmen,
with refugees from various other tribes. The Society
had been at work among them for twenty years with
some success, and the community had chosen as their
chief a Christian Bushman named Waterboer, who
conducted their affairs with great discretion and fidelity.
Under his rule the Griquas became a power to be
reckoned with on the border, and on one critical occasion they were the means of averting disaster from
the Colony. In Griqua Town Mary Moffat was born,
who afterwards became the wife of David Livingstone. After her birth Moffat, or Mosheté as the
natives called him, became known as Ra-Mary (father
of Mary), while his wife, by the same native usage,
was designated Ma-Mary.

IV : *The Romance of Kuruman*

The Moffats now proceeded to Kuruman which will
be for ever associated with their life and labours. The
settlement depended for its existence on the water of
the Kuruman River so called, though it was a fountain
rather than a running stream. Westward the land
rapidly faded into the desert, while eastward it grew
more fertile towards the Transvaal. The Bechuanas
were still in unbroken heathenism. "They looked at
the sun with the eyes of an ox." Christian truth was

received with stolid indifference or with shouts of derisive laughter. "Our labours," writes Moffat, "might well be compared to the attempts of a child to grasp the surface of a polished mirror, or those of a husbandman labouring to transform the surface of a granite rock into arable land, on which he might sow his seed." The rude hut of the missionaries gave them none of the privacy of home life, for men and women would crowd into it as often and as long as they had a mind, and, to make matters worse, they never lost a chance of pilfering. One of themselves fitly described their condition when he said to Moffat years afterwards, "You found us beasts, not men."

A long continued drought made the situation more difficult, for the missionaries were suspected of frustrating the efforts of the official rainmaker. The earnest looks which they were seen to cast towards the sky whenever a cloud appeared were sufficient evidence that they bewitched the rain. They were ordered by the chiefs to leave the country under threats of violence, to which the fearless answer was given, "You may shed our blood or burn us out. Then shall they who sent us know, and God who now sees and hears what we do, shall know, that we have been persecuted indeed." These solemn words awed their opponents, and in the end the rainmaker was the first to go.

In 1823 vague and disturbing rumours began to reach Kuruman of a savage horde of warriors advancing from the east, and spreading universal destruction along their path. They proved to be the Mantiti, a branch of the Zulu family, which, like the Matabele, had broken bounds and become the scourge of every tribe they encountered. Moffat, who at first did not re-gard these rumours seriously, took a journey to the northeast to visit the Bangwaketsi. As he advanced he soon had convincing evidence that a fearful danger was imminently threatening the Bechuanas and Kuruman. He hurried home and a meeting of chiefs and people was hastily summoned. Great was the consternation, and some proposed flight into the Kalahari Desert. To Moffat the only hope seemed to lie in the horses and guns of the Griquas and, his proposal being agreed to, he proceeded to Griqua Town to solicit their help. The Griquas, seeing their own safety imperilled, responded promptly to the appeal and brought to Kuruman a force of a hundred mounted men. Joining forces with the Bechuanas they advanced to meet the enemy. The hordes of the Mantiti came surging onward and refused every attempt at negotiation. They fought with in-credible ferocity and scattered the Bechuanas like chaff. But the horses and guns of the Griquas, with which they were totally unacquainted, struck terror into their ranks and they broke and fled. But for this check they would without doubt have overrun the northern districts of Cape Colony.

Moffat's conduct throughout this crisis made a deep and lasting impression upon the natives, and gave him a prestige among them which he never afterwards lost. For some time the country continued in a very unset-tled state. The scattered hordes of the Mantiti still roamed about, while lawless bands of Griquas took to the trade of freebooters and terrorised the tribes. On one occasion Moffat had an escape which he regarded as singularly providential. He had gone to the north to visit the Bangwaketsi, and a considerable number of Griquas travelled with him for the purpose of elephant hunting. They were to return home by different routes but at the last moment the Griquas, for no apparent reason, determined to return with Moffat. On the way they were attacked by a strong force of Mantiti, into whose hands Moffat would undoubtedly have fallen had he been alone.

Amid these alarms the work of the mission was steadily carried on, but still the heathenism of the people presented an unbroken front. There were many dark hours of despondency but faith triumphed. "We may not live to see it," Mary Moffat would say to her husband, "but the awakening will come as surely as the sun will rise to-morrow." Weak in body and naturally prone to depression and gloomy fears, she had an unwavering confidence in the future of God's work. Writing to a friend who had asked if there was anything she could send out for the use of the mission, Mrs. Moffat said, "Send us a communion service. We shall want it one day." Two or three years elapsed, and so fruitless did the work appear that the Directors of the Society were considering the advisability of abandoning the mission.

At length in 1829 the first clear signs of daybreak appeared. The services in the little mission church began to be crowded and a new interest and emotion seemed to awaken in heathen breasts. The record of it may best be given in Moffat's own words. "The simple Gospel," he writes, "now melted their flinty hearts, and eyes now wept which never before shed the tear of hallowed sorrow. Notwithstanding our earnest desires and fervent prayers, we were taken by surprise. We had so long been accustomed to indifference, that we felt unprepared to look on a scene which perfectly overwhelmed our minds. Our temporary little chapel became a Bochim—a place of weeping—and the sympathy of feeling spread from heart to heart, so that even infants wept. Some, after gazing with extreme intensity of feeling on the preacher, would fall down in hysterics, and others were carried out in a state of great exhaustion." After instruction and examination Moffat baptised his first six converts and partook with them of the sacrament of the Lord's Supper. "Our feelings on that occasion," he writes, "were such as our pen would fail to describe. We were as those that dreamed, while we realised the promise on which our souls had often hung, 'He that goeth forth and weepeth, bearing precious seed, shall doubtless come again with rejoicing, bringing his sheaves with him.' " By a striking coincidence, the communion vessels which Mrs. Moffat had asked for years before, arrived on the Friday preceding that memorable Sunday.

V: *The Matabele*

The same year Moffat paid his first visit to the Matabele. For some time rumours had reached him of this powerful and warlike people, who were at that time settled beside the Limpopo, far to the east of Kuruman. They had come north from Zululand, and they afterwards overran the country as far as the Zambesi before their military despotism was broken by British arms.

Their chief, Mosilikatse, anxious to learn of the white man and his ways, sent two of his headmen to Kuruman. They were greatly struck by what they saw, and pressed Moffat to visit their chief. He consented, and after a long and arduous journey reached the kraal of the Matabele king. Mosilikatse gave him a cordial welcome and handsomely acknowledged the kindness shown to his deputies as kindness shown to himself. "My father," he said, "you have made my heart as white as milk. I cannot cease to wonder at the love of a stranger."

Moffat on his part was much struck with the military discipline of the Matabele and the savage pomp of their king. It exceeded anything that was to be seen elsewhere in South Africa. A tragic example was given of the spirit of the warriors. One of the Indunas, being condemned to death, was pardoned on the intercession of Moffat but sentenced to be disgraced from his rank. At once he besought the king to let him die like a warrior for he could not live in disgrace. His request was granted and he was led forth to instant execution. Such was the missionary's first Sunday morning among the Matabele.

Soon after Moffat's return to Kuruman he travelled to Cape Town with his wife and children, in order to put the children to school and at the same time to arrange for the printing of some parts of the New Testament which he had translated into Sechuana. Throughout his whole career he occupied every spare moment of a busy life with translation work and never ceased till he had given the Bechuanas the whole of the

Scriptures in their own language. Finding no printer in Cape Town to undertake the work he took it in hand himself under the guidance of a Government printer. This proved a fortunate circumstance for at that juncture a mission printing press arrived at the Cape, which enabled Moffat henceforth to do his own printing at Kuruman. The work of the mission was now proceeding hopefully. Schools were established at various centres with the help of native teachers, and pleasing evidences began to appear of a desire for improvement. Habits of personal cleanliness, greater decency in clothing, better houses and rude attempts at furniture were all welcome as signs of a new spirit among the people. A demand arose for candles, and the fat which had before been larded on to greasy bodies was now put to a better use. Everywhere the people were keen to learn the mystery of reading. To meet this ardour Moffat taught them to sing the ABC to the tune of *Auld Lang Syne,* but he confesses that sometimes, when it was rendered far on into the night, he "was ready to wish it at John o' Groat's House." In 1835 Moffat again visited the Matabele and spent two months with Mosilikatse, who showed him round the country, travelling in Moffat's wagon. The corpulent monarch found the bed in the wagon much to his taste and invited its owner to come and lie beside him, an invitation which was politely declined. Soon after this visit the Matabele, being attacked by the Zulus and feeling also the pressure of the Boers in the Transvaal, migrated to the north where for some years they were lost sight of.

VI :   *Moffat and Livingstone*

The Moffats had now been twenty years in Africa and had endured to the full the privations and hardships that fall to the lot of the pioneer. Though still in early middle life they were veterans in the service and their work had impressed the imagination of the home Churches to a degree they had little idea of. In 1838 they came home on their first and only furlough. As happens in such a case with a popular missionary, Moffat immediately found himself overwhelmed with engagements. The clamorous public demanded its hero on every possible occasion, and his own ardent spirit made him only too willing to respond. Amid such distractions Moffat found time to see through the press the Sechuana New Testament and to publish an account of his experiences under the title of *"Labours and Scenes in South Africa."* The most notable event of this visit, however, was the securing of a powerful recruit for the Bechuana mission in the person of David Livingstone, who sailed for the Cape in 1840, taking with him 500 copies of Moffat's Sechuana New Testament. The Moffats followed in 1842. Their visit to the home country, following, as it did, immediately after the visit of John Williams from the South Seas, gave a powerful stimulus to missionary effort in all the Churches.

The return to Kuruman, in its concluding stages, assumed the appearance of a triumphal procession. Livingstone met the Moffats at the Vaal to help them across the river, and from that point onwards the villagers poured out with boisterous welcome. Chiefs and tribesmen from far and near came to visit their old friends whom they had hardly expected to see again. Among these a specially welcome visitor was Mothibi, the paramount chief of the Bechuanas who had but recently, in his old age, professed the Christian faith.

Now commenced a second term of service which continued without a break for twenty-seven years till Moffat's retirement in 1870. During this period his fame was gradually overshadowed by the supreme romance and glory of Livingstone, but the achievements of the older man were very notable and he retained to the end the adventurous spirit of his youth. Livingstone went to open a new station, 250 miles north of Kuruman, to which he soon after brought his bride, the younger Mary Moffat. In the subsequent explorations of Livingstone Moffat naturally took a deep interest. They were entirely in accord with his own views. He had long felt that the missionary advance northward from the Cape had reached its limit. "I feel persuaded," he wrote in 1840, "that the period has arrived when we must abandon the idea of long, expensive, tiresome, and in some instances dangerous journeys, either from the promontory of the Cape, or from Algoa Bay, to remote distances in the interior. It is now quite time to look to the eastern and western coasts of the continent, and form a chain of stations from either or both, towards the centre." From these words it will be seen that Livingstone was following no hasty and impulsive scheme of his own.

Another determining factor in the situation was the hostility of the Boers. They had deliberately resolved to cut the chain of mission stations which stretched towards the north between Transvaal and the Kalahari Desert, and thus bar the way to the interior. In face of this policy Moffat therefore felt that Livingstone's journeys were a vital necessity if the Gospel was to be carried to the teeming millions of Central Africa.

Meantime at Kuruman the arduous routine work of a mission station went on steadily from year to year. In many respects the second stage of work in a mission field is more trying than the first, for the upward progress of a heathen people is wavering and painfully slow. Converts suffer, in many cases, grievous relapse, and even when they continue steadfast their conceptions of the Christian life are very frequently disappointing. So we find Moffat writing sorrowfully in 1851, "We are instant in season and out of season in our public duties and in the work of translation, but the progress is slow, very slow." Mary Moffat also, writing to her father, says, "There is much to discourage, yet we feel we must not despair." Very sensibly she recalls the state of the people thirty years before, and reckons up the progress already made. Such thoughts having passed through her mind as she sat in the little native prayer meeting and listened to the singing of the Bechuana Christians, she adds, "I came home stronger in my hopes and expectations for the kingdom of Christ in poor Africa than I had been for some months."

In 1853 Moffat paid his third visit to the Matabele who now occupied the country up to the Zambesi. He found Mosilikatse, the once proud warrior king, now an aged cripple, and was fortunately able to restore in some measure his shattered health. One object of this journey was to convey supplies to the Zambesi for Livingstone who had gone into the unknown interior the previous year. Finding it impossible to reach the Zambesi in his wagon Moffat procured Matabele carriers who went forward with the supplies. On reaching the river they left the packages on the bank as the natives could not be induced to come over and receive them. After the departure of the Matabele, however, the timid river folk stored the goods carefully on an island where Livingstone found them all safe on his arrival from the west coast.

Moffat returned to Kuruman and resumed his work of preaching and teaching, translating and printing. Meantime Livingstone, having reached the west coast at Loanda, recrossed the continent to the east coast and carried home to England the story of his discoveries. The great interest aroused by his unparalleled journey led to an expansion of missionary enterprise. The attention of the London Missionary Society was directed to the Matabele on the south side of the Zambesi, and to the Makololo, on the north side of the river. Two missionary expeditions were fitted out to commence work among these tribes. It was proposed that Moffat should lead the expedition to the Matabele, as his influence with Mosilikatse would do much to pave the way. This was in 1857, when Moffat was sixty-two years of age and had forty-one years of service behind him. Far from refusing this new call he set off at once to prepare the Matabele for the arrival of the mission. It meant a seven hundred mile trek to the northeast, through a thirsty and difficult country, and the task before him was no easy one. Mosilikatse had confidence in Moffat but of strangers he was suspicious. Isolation had for long been the policy of the Matabele. They feared, not without reason, that the advent of the white man would be the beginning of the end. Moffat, having overcome these scruples and obtained a reluctant consent to the establishment of the mission, now hurried south to Cape Town to meet the new missionaries and to say good-bye to Livingstone who was going out to his post as British consul on the Zambesi. Among the missionaries for Matabele land was Moffat's own son John, whose salary for five years was guaranteed by Livingstone. To him Mrs. Moffat wrote feelingly, "On the tenth of next month it will be twenty-five years since I parted with your father when he visited the tyrant Mosilikatse the second time, he being then the terror of the tribes in the latitudes north of us, and it was deemed prudent to conciliate him that the interior might not be closed against the progress of the Gospel. How little did I then think that the very babe who sat before me on his nurse's lap was destined to go to that savage people to hold before them the lamp of eternal life. Unable as I then was to hold you in my embrace, your sweet smiles, which in my solitude I so often witnessed, are yet engraven on my now shattered memory. Methinks they said, 'Cheer up, dear mother, though you think your course is nearly finished, I am destined to live to fulfil your heart's desire.' "

In 1859 the expeditions to the Makololo and the Matabele set out from Kuruman. The Makololo mission was a disastrous failure and forms one of the most tragic episodes in missionary history. The mission to the Matabele was established only by the influence and efforts of Moffat who spent a year with that war-like people, soothing their suspicions and organising the mission station at Inyati. His activities are thus described by one who witnessed them. "There were houses to be built, wagons to be repaired, garden ground to be broken up. Early and late Moffat was to be found at work, always at work, it might be at the saw-pit, or the blacksmith's forge, or the carpenter's bench, or aiding the younger men where their own knowledge and skill failed them." Having completed his work he took his last leave of Mosilikatse and returned to Kuruman.

VII: *Farewell to Kuruman*

The closing years of Moffat's life in Africa were as busy and arduous as any, though less romantic and adventurous. His failing strength made long journeys impossible, and he confined his energies to administering the affairs of the central station, while younger colleagues went farther afield. His name was a household word among all the tribes north of the Orange River, many of whom believed him to be the paramount chief of the white men. Unscrupulous traders, taking advantage of this, represented themselves as his agents, delivered messages in his name, and declared that they dared not face their great chief at Kuruman unless they got more ivory and better prices for their goods.

The home at Kuruman was shadowed again and again

by heavy sorrows. In 1862 the Moffats' eldest son Robert died when on a wagon journey, only a few hours distant from Kuruman. About the same time the sad news arrived of the death of Mrs. Livingstone on the Zambesi. In 1865 Moffat himself was savagely attacked by a crazy native armed with a knobkerry who struck him some terrible blows that endangered his life. It was months before he recovered from the shock. Next year M. Frédoux, a French missionary who had married Ann Moffat, met his death under tragic circumstances. He was endeavouring to reason with a trader whose atrocious conduct had roused the hostility of the natives, when the desperate man blew up his own wagon which was loaded with gunpowder, instantly killing Frédoux and himself and a dozen natives.

The long day of service was drawing to a close. In 1868 Moffat was joined by his son John, at Kuruman, in whose care he was happy to think he would leave his beloved work. The Directors had for some time been urging him to come home, and he now felt that his strength was no longer equal to his task. In 1870 he took his last farewell of the people among whom he had laboured for more than half a century, and by whom he was now regarded with feelings of deepest veneration. The scene is thus described by his son. "On Sunday the twentieth of March Robert Moffat preached for the last time in the Kuruman church. In all that great congregation there were few of his own contemporaries. The older people were for the most part children at the time when they had first seen the missionaries. With a pathetic grace peculiarly his own, he pleaded with those who still remained unbelieving amid the Gospel privileges they had now enjoyed so many years. With a fatherly benediction he commended to the grace of God those who had been to him a joy and crown. It was an impressive close to an impressive career. On Friday following, the departure took place. The final scene was such as could scarcely be described in words. As the old missionary and his wife came out of their door and walked to their wagon they were beset by the crowds, each longing for one more touch of the hand and one more word. As the wagon drove away it was followed by all who could walk, and a long and pitiful wail rose, enough to melt the hardest heart."

Amid the universal sadness it must have been an inspiration for the two veterans to reflect on the contrast between the manner of their departure and the reception they met with on their first arrival. Few workers in the Kingdom of God are privileged to see so profound a change produced as the result of their labours. It is the rich reward sometimes given to those who have gone forth in faith into the wilderness of heathenism, to sow the seed, to tend and water it, until at last they gather in abundance the rich fruits of the garden of God.

VIII: *A Missionary to the Last*

A few sentences may suffice to give an outline of the last years of Moffat's life. It is proof of the extraordinary vitality of the man that, having come home after so arduous a life, he continued his services to the missionary cause with great activity for thirteen years. Even the death of his wife in 1872, though it made him feel very desolate and homeless, did not crush his spirit. He travelled extensively in England and Scotland on missionary deputation work, and once he went as far as Paris, where he addressed several meetings, notably a great gathering of 4000 French Protestant children. Everywhere he went his presence excited the strongest interest, for he had come to be regarded by universal consent as "the venerable father of the missionary world." Various honours were conferred on him, including an audience with Queen Victoria. Several thousand pounds were subscribed for a Training Institute at Kuruman, and Moffat himself received a gift of £5000. On one of his journeys to Scotland he visited the home of his boyhood, where he had some amusing encounters with his old school fellows. Not without difficulty did he convince them that he was really "the great Moffat."

"Are you aware, sir," said the village tailor oracularly, "that if you are really the person you represent yourself to be, you must be the father-in-law of Livingstone, the African explorer."

"And so I am," said Moffat.

The old tailor got to his feet. "Is it possible," he exclaimed, "that the father-in-law of Livingstone stands before me, and under my humble roof?"

In 1874 the body of Livingstone was brought home to England and interred in Westminster Abbey. Moffat escorted the remains from Southampton to London and was present at the funeral service in the Abbey. To him it was a deeply affecting occasion, and must have brought a rush of memories out of the heroic past, of African travel and toil.

His last days were spent at Park Cottage, Leigh, where, tended by the loving care of his daughter, he died on August 10, 1883. Many tributes were paid to his memory and the value of his work. The following sentences from a leading article in the *Times* may serve to indicate the nation's estimate of his life. "Dr. Robert Moffat has left an abiding name as a pioneer of modern missionary work in South Africa. . . . It is the fashion in some quarters to scoff at missionaries, to receive their reports with incredulity, to look at them at the best as no more than harmless enthusiasts, proper subjects for pity, if not for ridicule. The records of missionary work in South Africa must be a blank page to those by whom such ideas are entertained. We owe it to our missionaries that the whole region has been opened up. . . . The progress of South Africa has been mainly due to men of Moffat's stamp. It would seem indeed that it is only by the agency of such men as Moffat and his like that the contact of the white and black races can be anything but a curse to the blacks. . . . Moffat's name will be remembered while the South African Church endures, and his example will remain with us as a stimulus to others, and as an abiding proof of what a Christian missionary can be and can do."

CHAPTER III

David Livingstone, the most famous of the missionary heroes of Africa and the prince of African explorers, was born at Blantyre on the Clyde on the tenth of March, 1813. He came of highland ancestry, his great grandfather having fallen at the Battle of Culloden, but it would be a mistake to seek here, as some have done, the master key to Livingstone's character. His Highland pride is but another name for Scottish independence, while his strong common sense and pawky humour, his resoluteness, his sturdy democratic principles, are characteristic of the Saxon more than of the Gael.

I: *Blantyre Mill*

His father was an itinerant tea dealer who, being a man of ardent religious zeal, acted the part of an unpaid colporteur. His mother is described as "a delicate little woman with a wonderful flow of good spirits, and remarkable for the beauty of her eyes, to which those of her son David bore a strong resemblance." The two-roomed house in Blantyre must have been sadly overcrowded as five children grew up in it, but it was a home where the sterling Christian character of the parents, the mother's gentleness blending with the father's strictness, impressed upon their children's minds the fear of God.   The boys had to begin work early in order to contribute to the support of the family. Accordingly at the age of ten David was sent to the cotton mill which stands on the bank of the Clyde, a stone's throw from his home.

His hours of work were from 6 a.m. to 8 p.m., and after that he would rush off to an evening school from 8 to 10.   Returning home he often pursued his studies till midnight, when his mother would snatch away his book and pack him off to bed.   From an early age his ambition was to become a medical missionary in China. With this end in view he attended classes in Glasgow during the winter season and returned to his loom in Blantyre mill for the summer.   "I never received a farthing of aid from anyone," he wrote afterwards, "and should have accomplished my project of going to China as a medical missionary in the course of time by my own efforts, had not some friends advised my joining the London Missionary Society on account of its perfectly unsectarian character."

His application to the Society being favourably entertained, he was summoned to London for examination.   While there he went with a fellow-student to visit Westminster Abbey.   How little could he have dreamed as he gazed around him at the monuments of the mighty dead that he was standing upon his own grave! Meantime war with China had closed that door and Livingstone's thoughts now began to turn towards Africa. This was due mainly to the influence of Dr. Moffat who had come home on furlough and was powerfully stirring the churches by his addresses and writings. After several talks with him Livingstone said, "What is the use of my waiting for the end of this abominable opium war? I will go at once to Africa!" He sailed for the Cape on the 8th of December, 1840. It was very characteristic of him that the three months' voyage was mainly spent in learning from the captain of the ship as much as possible of the art of navigation. "He was very obliging to me," writes Livingstone, "and gave me all the information in his power respecting the use of the quadrant, frequently sitting up till twelve o'clock at night for the purpose of taking lunar observations with me."

II: *The Valley of Mabotsa*

Livingstone's instructions from the London Missionary Society were to proceed to Kuruman and from there to prospect for the opening of a new mission station among the tribes to the north. After various journeys he selected "the beautiful valley of Mabotsa," and thither he removed in 1843. It was while at Mabotsa that he was attacked by a wounded lion and only rescued by the courage of his native teacher, Mebalwé, and another man whose life he had previously saved. His left arm, however, was shattered above the elbow, producing a false joint. It is one of the most amazing facts in the story of Livingstone that through all his subsequent labours and mighty wanderings he was a crippled man, with one arm so maimed that it was painful to lift a gun or raise his left hand to his head.

He soon found a comforter, for on going to Kuruman to recruit his health he became engaged to Dr. Moffat's eldest daughter, Mary. They were married shortly afterwards and spent at Mabotsa the first happy year of their married life. In 1846 the Livingstones moved to Chonuane, where was the kraal of Sechele, the chief cf the Bakwains. Drought, however, soon compelled the removal of the tribe to Kolobeng, which was Livingstone's home till he set out on his great journey across Africa in 1852. It was the only home he ever had, and when, twenty years after, in his lonely wanderings, he looked back to it with fond longing, he felt but one pang of regret, that he had not played with his children more when he had them, now he had none to play with. He had usually been so tired at night, he says pathetically, that there was no fun left in him.

The chief, Sechele, on first hearing the Gospel, was much affected and asked Livingstone, "How is it that your forefathers did not send to my forefathers news of these things sooner?" Surely a pertinent question, and one not easily answered. He became an eager learner, and in 1848 made open profession of his Christian faith. His subsequent career, however, rendered that profession of doubtful value, for, though he became extraordinarily well versed in Scripture and preached with earnestness, he still persisted in some heathen practices. The spirit of Livingstone's ministry may be gathered from a sentence in a letter to his father, written in July, 1848. "For a long time I felt much depressed after preaching the unsearchable riches of Christ to apparently insensible hearts, but now I like to dwell on the love of the great Mediator, for it always warms my own heart, and I know that the Gospel is the power of God, the great means that He employs for the regeneration of our ruined world." It may be said, once for all, that he held this conviction to the last, and never ceased to be a missionary-preacher of this evangel.

During this period Livingstone's eyes were continually directed towards the north. The country around Kolobeng was barren and thinly populated, while the security of the inhabitants was threatened from the east and northeast by the Boers and the Matabele. There were reports of more fertile and populous regions beyond the Kalahari Desert to the north, where a powerful chief, Sebituane, had established himself. Sechele was willing to remove his tribe thither if it were found feasible. No doubt also Livingstone had a laudable ambition to be the first white man to reach the rumoured lake in the interior, which up till then had baffled repeated and determined attempts of explorers from the Cape.

Accordingly he set out from Kolobeng with two English hunters, Mr. Oswell and Mr. Murray, and after an arduous journey across the desert reached Lake Ngami on August 1, 1849. The discovery of this lake, though eclipsed by Livingstone's subsequent achievements, was a remarkable feat, and gained for him a grant from the Royal Geographical Society. A vague impression prevailed that the centre of Africa was one vast desert. The Kalahari was spoken of as the Southern Sahara. Yet here, in the heart of it, was an extensive fresh water lake, with a fine river watering a fertile plain. Sebituane's country, however, was still farther to the north. Next year Livingstone again set out from Kuruman, with his wife and children and Mr. Oswell, but owing to fever they were not able to penetrate beyond Lake Ngami.

A third attempt, in 1851, was successful, and resulted in the discovery of a glorious river, known to the natives as the Sesheke or Liambai, which proved to be the upper Zambesi. Here Sebituane had established himself and ruled over a wide domain. His career had been a romantic one. Born in Basutoland, he was one of the leaders of the wild horde of Mantiti who were routed at Kuruman by the Griquas in 1821. Pursuing his way north with a shattered remnant of his people, the Makololo as they came to be called, he conquered the Barotsi who inhabited the wide valley of the Zambesi, and imposèd on them the language of the Basutos. This afterwards had a remarkable influence in leading to the evangelisation of the country by M. Coillard.

Sebituane gave Livingstone a hearty welcome, but very shortly afterwards he took ill and died. Livingstone was deeply moved by his death, both on personal grounds and because it seemed to imperil the vast enterprise which had now taken definite shape in his mind and became, henceforth, the master passion of his life.

III: *The Road to the North*

This enterprise was the opening up of Central Africa to civilisation and the Gospel. Various influences, acting on his mind since he landed in Africa, had combined to turn his thoughts in this direction, till at last it grew to an invincible conviction that here was the divinely appointed path for him. For one thing, he early took the view that the number of missionaries in the Colony was excessive in proportion to the population and in view of the vast needs of Africa. In 1843 we find him making strong representations to the London Missionary Society on the subject. He held that the European missionary should continually advance to the occupation of new fields, leaving his work to be followed up by native teachers. This policy was opposed by many missionaries of experience, and it must be admitted that time has not altogether confirmed Livingstone's high estimate of the efficiency of the native teacher, and especially of his power to work alone.

Another influence was the difficulty of transport. Pondering the problem of a farther advance into the interior, Livingstone could not but see, as Moffat had seen before him, that the limit of expansion northward from the Cape had been reached. No Cape to Cairo railway was then so much as dreamed of, and the tedious ox wagon, consuming months in the journey from Cape Town, and now faced with the terrible Kalahari Desert, obviously could do no more. Accordingly we find Livingstone writing in 1850, "When we burst through the barrier on the north, it appeared very plain that no mission could be successful there, unless we could get a well watered country having a passage to the sea on either the east or west coast. This project I am almost afraid to meet, but nothing else will do."

Another determining influence was the attitude of the Boers of the Transvaal. It may appear incredible that men calling themselves Protestant Christians, descendants also of the persecuted Church of the Netherlands, should have acted as these Boers did. But they were, in the main, composed of the most ignorant and brutal elements of the Dutch colonists, who had trekked into the wilds to escape from contact with civilisation. They believed themselves to be God's chosen people, and the natives they regarded as the Canaanites, to be dispossessed, slaughtered and enslaved. There was a vague impression among them that the Promised Land was somewhere to the north and might one day be reached by their wagons. With such views they became the determined opponents of missions to the natives, and were resolved to close the road to the north both to the missionary and to the trader. Accordingly they ordered the Bechuanas to stop all white travellers going through their country and threatened to attack any tribe that would receive a native teacher. "The Boers," writes Livingstone, "resolved to shut up the interior, and I determined to open the country, and we shall see who have been most successful in resolution—they or I." Truly we shall see.

Being thus resolved, Livingstone returned to Kolobeng to make preparations for his great adventure. First he travelled to Cape Town with his family to send them home to Scotland, and to procure necessary supplies for himself. When Mrs. Livingstone and the four children sailed from Cape Town on April 23, 1852, Livingstone saw the final breaking up of his home. Malicious tongues whispered in after years that his home life had never been happy, a slander which caused both him and his wife the keenest pain. The following letter, written shortly after their separation, may be quoted for its exquisite beauty and to show the tenderness of their love."

"My dearest Mary, How I miss you now, and the dear children! My heart yearns incessantly over you. You have been a great blessing to me. May God bless you for all your kindnesses! I see no face now to be compared to that sunburnt one which has so often greeted me with its kind looks. Let us do our duty to our Saviour, and we shall meet again. I wish that time were now. You may read the letters over again which I wrote at Mabotsa, the sweet time you know. As I told you before, I tell you again, they are true, true. There is not a bit of hypocrisy in them. I never show all my feelings, but I can say truly, my dearest, that I loved you when I married you, and the longer I lived with you, I loved you the better. . . . Take the children round you and kiss them for me. Tell them I have left them for the love of Jesus, and they must love him too."

Not every husband would bid his wife read over again his old love letters, and stand to every word of them, nor are there many wives, perhaps, who would break into a rapturous poetic welcome on their husband's return, as did Mary Moffat when Livingstone came home in 1856.

On the 8th of June Livingstone left the Cape in his wagon and reached Kuruman at the end of August. Here he was detained by the breaking of a wagon wheel—fortunately, as it proved. For news arrived that the Boers, under Pretorius, had attacked

Kolobeng, burned the town and killed or captured the people. Had Livingstone been at home at the time of the attack he would probably have been killed, for Pretorius had threatened to take his life. He would certainly have lost all his stores. The Boers left his home a wreck. "My house," he writes, "which had stood perfectly secure for years under the protection of the natives, was plundered. . . . The books of a good library—my solace in our solitude,—were not taken away, but handfuls of the leaves were torn out and scattered over the place. My stock of medicines was smashed, and all our furniture and clothing carried off and sold at public auction to pay the expenses of the foray."

After this outrage Livingstone was more determined than ever "to open a path through the country or perish!" Leaving Kuruman and making a wide détour to the west to avoid the Boers, he once more crossed the Kalahari Desert and in June, 1853, reached Linyanti, the capital of the Makololo country. It is situated on the Chobe, a tributary of the Zambesi, about a hundred miles south of that river. Here Livingstone was welcomed by Sekeletu, the son of his old friend Sebituane, and he speedily acquired great influence over the young chief and his people. After a month spent at Linyanti he persuaded Sekeletu to accompany him on a tour through the Barotsi country. Having crossed the intervening flat, they struck the Zambesi at Sesheke, some miles west of where the town of Livingstone now stands, and embarking in canoes they sailed a considerable distance up the river. No healthy site for a mission station, however, could be found. The whole country was a vast plain, inundated annually by the river, and choked with rank vegetation which made it unhealthy at all seasons. After nine weeks a return was made to Linyanti. Of his experiences at this time Livingstone wrote, "I have been, during a nine weeks' tour, in closer contact with heathenism than I had ever been before, and though all, including the chief, were as kind and attentive to me as possible, yet to endure the dancing, roaring, and singing, the jesting, anecdotes, grumbling, quarrelling, and murdering of these children of nature, seemed more like a severe penance than anything I had before met with in the course of my missionary duties. I took thence a more intense disgust at heathenism than before, and formed a greatly elevated opinion of the latent effects of missions in the south, among tribes which are reported to have been as savage as the Makololo."

IV : *Crossing the Continent*

The more daring scheme of opening a way to the west coast caught the imagination of Sekeletu and his people, and it should never be forgotten that only by their help was Livingstone enabled to cross the continent. After discussion in the tribal assembly twenty-seven men were appointed to accompany him. They became famous as his Makololo, but he more correctly calls them Zambesians, for only two of the number were genuine Makololo, the rest were Barotsi and other natives of the valley. The plan proposed by Livingstone was to ascend the Zambesi as far as possible, and from its head waters to strike northwest to

Loanda on the coast. A nearer point on the coast was Benguela, but in that direction Portuguese slave traders had been active, and Livingstone knew it to be dangerous to follow in their track.

The journey from Linyanti to Loanda occupied six and a half months, from November 11, 1853, to May 31, 1854. It was the greatest feat of African travel yet accomplished, and displayed to the full Livingstone's extraordinary qualities as an explorer. His journal records an interminable succession of tribes and villages, never before visited by a white man. After ascending the Zambesi and the Leeba by canoe the carriers advanced on foot, while Livingstone rode as much as possible on oxback. The rainy season had now set in and they found immense flats where the water stood knee deep in the grass. Some of these were as much as twenty miles in width. Across these flats they had perforce to wade, sometimes for days on end, under pitiless rain and with an occasional flooded river to swim. Throughout the whole journey Livingstone suffered from recurrent attacks of fever, and sometimes lay in his hut unconscious. He has been blamed for gross disregard of his health, in travelling without proper camp equipment, subsisting on native food, and often sleeping on the ground in wet clothes. It may be replied that he had to do his work with the resources at his disposal, and no other traveller, even with the best of equipment, has equalled his record. Careless he was not, nor slow to learn by experience. Having felt the chilling, depressing influence of heavy rain, especially upon the naked bodies of the men, he taught them to take shelter or to make a rude thatch of grass for their backs when the rain came on, and had fewer cases of fever in consequence. "A missionary," he wrote, "must never forget that, in the tropics, he is an exotic plant. In a hot climate efficiency mainly depends on husbanding the resources."

The tribes through whose country he passed were in general disposed to be friendly when treated with courtesy and enlightened as to the object of the journey. Some, however, were tyrannous and threatening. It has been claimed for Livingstone, as the brightest star in his crown, that he crossed Africa without firing an angry shot. There were moments on this journey when that record came perilously near being broken. Sometimes a demand was made for "a gun, an ox, or a man." Occasionally an ox had to be surrendered, but Livingstone declared that before he would sell one of his men they would all die together. He was no pacifist. "We would do almost anything," he says, "to avoid a collision with degraded natives, but in the case of an invasion— our blood boils at the very thought of our wives, daughters, or sisters being touched—we, as men with human feelings, would unhesitatingly fight to the death, with all the fury in our power."

Throughout these trials and perils the Makololo behaved admirably on the whole. Only once, when Livingstone was down with fever, did some of them show a spirit of mutiny, but his sudden appearance from the hut, haggard and angry, with his pistols in his hands, quelled the malcontents in a moment. In the Chiboque country a hostile chief tried to pick a quarrel by alleging that one of the carriers, in spitting, had touched one of his people. Extravagant demands were made for compensation, and savage warriors danced round threateningly. Livingstone sat with his double-barrelled gun across his knees, ready to fire at the first attack. At length, by patience and tact and the peace-offering of an ox, the danger was surmounted. As they neared Portuguese territory the local chiefs became more troublesome in their demands. They had been accustomed to exact tribute from the slave traders who, being encumbered with gangs of unwilling captives, were glad to pay a heavy price for permission to proceed coastwise with their booty. These traders, though called Portuguese, were half-castes with woolly hair. Livingstone's men were careful to point out to the natives that he alone was a genuine specimen of "the white men who come out of the sea." "Look at his hair," they said, "washed straight by the water!"

A steep descent from the plateau of the interior, through narrow glens, brought the travellers to the fine valley of the Quango. With some difficulty they crossed the river and set foot on Portuguese territory. Here they received a most kindly welcome from Cypriano, a young half-caste Portuguese sergeant of militia. This was the first instance of that warm hearted hospitality which Livingstone received from the Portuguese as he travelled down to the coast, a hospitality which did much to restore his shattered health, and which moved him to expressions of the deepest gratitude. At last the ocean came in sight. Unlike Xenophon's men, who hailed the familiar sight with joy, Livingstone's followers were struck dumb with awe. Describing their feelings afterwards they said, "We marched along with our father, believing that what the ancients had always told us was true, that the world has no end. But all at once the world said to us, 'I am finished, there is no more of me.' "

Livingstone entered Loanda little better than a walking skeleton, but he found a home in the house of Mr. Gabriel, the British consul, and in a few minutes was enjoying delicious sleep in an English bed. He afterwards had a severe and prolonged relapse, but on recovering he was thankful to find that he was free from lassitude and like his old self again. He was now offered a passage home in a British warship but he declined the tempting offer. He knew that the Makalolo would be quite unable to make their way back alone through the hostile tribes on the way, and he felt himself in honour bound to take them home to their chief. His journey also had proved that there was no practicable route for wagons to the west coast. He therefore resolved to return to the interior with the view of trying to find a path to the east coast by following the course of the Zambesi. As we shall see, this scrupulous honour in restoring his men to their homes had its exact counterpart and recompense when those who followed him in his last journey, led by two Zambesians, Susi and Chuma, carried his body for nine months to the coast, in order to deliver it to his people.

The return journey from Loanda to the interior occupied a year, from September, 1854, to September, 1855. A considerable part of that time, however, was spent in the hinterland of the Portuguese colony, where Livingstone, on hearing of the wreck of the mailboat in which he had sent home his letters, maps and journals, sat down and patiently reproduced the whole of them

before he buried himself once more in the wilds.   Then
he led his men homewards.   On reaching their own
people in Zambesi valley they had a great ovation, and
little wonder.   For had they not gone to the ends of
the earth and returned safe, with not a man missing?
In the neighbourhood of Sesheke Livingstone had the
pleasure of finding some packages of goods which Dr.
Moffat had succeeded in sending north a year before
by Matabele carriers and which had been safely stored
on an island in the river.   Sekeletu was delighted with
the results of the expedition, opening, as it did, the prospect of peaceful commerce with the white man.   He
therefore readily entered into Livingstone's plan of finding a path to the east coast by following the Zambesi
to the sea.

After six weeks spent in preparation, the new expedition started from Linyanti on November 3, 1855,
and the east coast was reached at Quilimane on May
21, 1856.   This second and more numerous caravan,
like the first, was equipped at the expense of the chief.
Livingstone cordially acknowledges this.   "The Makololo again fitted me out.   I was thus dependent on their
bounty, and that of other Africans, for the means of
going from Linyanti to Loanda, and again from Linyanti to the east coast, and I feel deeply grateful to
them."   No stronger proof could be given of Livingstone's extraordinary influence over the minds of the
Africans, and it must ever redound to their honour that
the greatest and most successful of all his journeys was
accomplished by their help alone.

Sekeletu convoyed Livingstone for the first part of
the way, and together they visited the Falls of the

Zambesi, a greater and in every respect more wonderful Niagara, as every traveller who has seen both will at once admit. Livingstone had heard from the natives the fame of the place "where smoke sounds," a place which they shunned with superstitious awe. Now he saw it for the first time and bestowed the name of the Victoria Falls. Here the mighty river, more than a mile wide, flowing through an open plain, is suddenly precipitated headlong into a narrow ravine, four hundred feet deep, where its waters are tortured and pulverised till clouds of steam rush up from the abyss, and tower in lofty pillars to the sky. How little could Livingstone have imagined that in less than fifty years the gorge would be bridged and the thunder of express trains would mingle with the solemn sound of the falling water! So swiftly fruitful has been his work of opening Central Africa.

The route chosen was along the north bank of the Zambesi, because on the map Tette, the farthest up-river setlement of the Portuguese, was erroneously marked as on that side of the river. Livingstone had therefore to cross the Kafue and the Loangwa, two considerable tributaries which flow from the north, and then he had to cross the Zambesi itself in order to reach Tette. As on the journey to Loanda, so here he found the tribes more hostile in the vicinity of Portuguese territory. At the crossing of the Loangwa the whole expedition seemed in imminent danger of annihilation. Livingstone passed a troubled night, as the following entry in his journal shows. "Felt much turmoil of spirit in view of having all my plans for the welfare of this great region and teeming population knocked on the head by savages to-morrow. But I read that Jesus came and said, 'All power is given unto me in heaven and in earth. Go yet therefore and teach all nations—and lo, *I am with you alway, even unto the end of the world.'* It is the word of a gentleman of the most sacred and strictest honour, and there's an end on't. I will not cross furtively by night as I intended. It would appear as flight, and should such a man as I flee? Nay, verily, I shall take observations for latitude and longitude to-night, though they may be the last. I feel quite calm now, thank God."

Once again faith was justified, tact and patience prevailed, and the crossing was made in safety. On reaching Tette Livingstone was received with the same kindness as he had experienced on the west coast at the hands of the Portuguese. Here he left his Makololo carriers, promising that only death would hinder his return from England to take them home again. Travelling down the river he reached the coast at Quilimane, and thus completed his great, transcontinental journey. It was an achievement such as could not have been considered possible till it was actually done, and when the whole circumstances are taken account of, it must be reckoned the greatest feat of exploration ever accomplished. One does not know which to admire most, the iron constitution and resolute will of the man, or his patient courtesy and good sense, or his sanity and humour, or his dauntless faith. All combined in a wonderful degree to make Livingstone the man he was and to enable him to do the work he did. It was said of him, even in his student days, "Fire, water, and a stone wall would not stop Livingstone in the fulfilment of any recognised duty." Yet with all his natural strength he could be infinitely patient and tactful, even when half delirious with fever; and at every step of the road he sought the guidance and grace of God. No text seems to have been more frequently in his mind than the words of the Psalm, "Commit thy way unto the Lord, trust also in Him, and He shall bring it to pass."

V: *Discouraged and Lionised*

At Quilimane Livingstone received a letter from the directors of the London Missionary Society informing him that they were restricted in aiding "plans only remotely connected with the spread of the Gospel," and that finances would not permit of the opening of a new field in the interior. It is easy to understand the scruples of the Directors. The Society's rules were not made to fit a Livingstone, any more than a hen run is built to fit an eagle, and it could not yet be foreseen how powerful an influence on missionary work Livingstone's travels were to exert. But naturally he felt deeply grieved and wrote to the secretary, "I had imagined in my simplicity that both my preaching, conversation, and travel were as nearly connected with the spread of the Gospel as the Boers would allow them to be. A plan of opening up a path from either the east or west coast for the teeming population of the interior was submitted to the judgment of the Directors, and received their formal approval. I have been seven times in peril of my life from savage men while laboriously and without swerving pursuing that plan, and never doubting that I was in the path of duty." He now felt that he must be free to do his work in his own way, under the strong conviction that he was so led of God. His relation with the Society, however, continued cordial, and when the mission to the Matabele was organised, Livingstone, now a British consul, made himself responsible for the salary of John Moffat, his brother-in-law, for five years, besides paying his outfit. This fact is witness, if witness be needed, that in Livingstone's life, from first to last, the missionary interest was supreme.

Livingstone reached London in December, 1856, and was at home till March, 1858. As was to be expected he was lionised in all circles, religious and political, scientific and commercial. Honours were showered upon him and he was hailed everywhere as the national hero. His book, *Travels and Researches in South Africa,* was a great success, and brought him in several thousands of pounds, most of which he devoted to the furtherance of his work. An appeal which he made at Cambridge led to the founding of the Universities' Mission. In February, 1858, he was appointed British consul for the east coast of Africa, and commander of an expedition for exploring Central Africa. This glittering hour of fame left him quite unspoiled, the same rugged, simple-hearted missionary he had been at Kolobeng. At a banquet given in his honour before he left England some reference was made to his wife, when Livingstone, addressing a most illustrious audience, said with great plainness, "My wife will accompany me in this expedition and will be most useful to me. She is able to work. She is willing to endure, and she well knows that in that country one must put one's hand to everything.   She knows that at the missionary's station the wife must be the maid of all work within, while the husband must be the jack of all trades without, and glad am I indeed that I am to be accompanied by my guardian angel."

VI: *Five Years on the Zambesi*

The expedition left England in March, 1858, and reached the mouth of the Zambesi on the 14th of May. Here they put together the little steamer, the *Ma-Robbert,* with which they were to navigate the river.   Livingstone was now to encounter difficultes and troubles to which he had previously been a stranger, and in addition there fell upon him and the cause he had at heart a succession of disasters.   His position as British consul did not smooth his way with the Portuguese authorities who began to suspect political aims, and, under secret orders from Portugal, did their utmost to obstruct his work.   Some friction arose among the members of the expedition, not all of whom shared his ideals. The naval officer in charge of the steamer resigned, and Livingstone himself was compelled to undertake the duties of navigation.   The steamer proved to be of wretched construction, and so utterly useless that Livingtsone sent home an order for another boat to be built at his own expense.   His two most loyal helpers were Dr. Kirk (afterwards Sir John Kirk) and Mr. E. D. Young of the Royal Navy.   With their aid he explored the course of the Shire, a tributary of the Zambesi which flows down from the south end of Lake Nyasa.   This led to the discovery of the Shire Highlands, the healthiest and most promising region yet found in Central Africa. Passing through these hills Livingstone, in successive journeys, discovered Lake Shirwa and Lake Nyasa, and was confirmed in his view that here was the finest field for missionary enterprise and commercial development. That this view was sound has been fully demonstrated since then, by the success of the Livingstonia Mission and the prosperity of Nyasaland.

Returning to the Zambesi Livingstone took the Makololo, or as many of them as wished to return, back to their home at Linyanti. Here, to his great grief, he learned that the mission party sent north from Kuruman to establish themselves among the Makololo, had been almost wiped out by fever. The story of this catastrophe is fully told by John Mackenzie, who rescued the survivors. Livingstone could not but feel that some responsibility rested on him, for the expedition had gone on his assurance of a friendly welcome from Sekeletu, and Sekeletu had shamefully robbed them and was even suspected of having poisoned them.

In the beginning of 1861 Livingstone was back at the coast to welcome Bishop Mackenzie and the pioneers of the Universities' Mission whom he helped to settle at Magomero in the Shire Highlands. But disaster was again in store. The Bishop, who seems to have been somewhat forceful in his methods, went to war with some slave-raiding tribes and blood was shed. Livingstone, with grave fears as to the future of the mission, went down to the mouth of the Zambesi to meet his wife who had come out to join him. With her came Bishop Mackenzie's sister and Mrs. Burrup, the wife of one of his colleagues. A young Scotsman, afterwards well known as Dr. Stewart of Lovedale, was also of the party, having been sent out to prospect for a suitable sphere for a Scottish mission. It was a happy and hopeful meeting, but the sky was speedily overcast. They had not gone far up the river when news came that Bishop Mackenzie and Mr. Burrup were both dead, and, soon after, the whole mission was withdrawn to Zanzibar. It was a deathblow to one of Livingstone's fondest hopes.

There followed a sorrow that touched him more deeply. He had found a temporary home for his wife in a Portuguese house at Shupanga, a pleasant spot on the summit of a rising ground that slopes up gently from the river on its southern bank. Here the long separated husband and wife spent a few happy weeks together. Livingstone wrote afterwards, "In our intercourse in private there was more than what would be thought by some a decorous amount of merriment and play. I said to her a few days before her fatal illness, 'We old bodies ought now to be more sober, and not play so much.' 'Oh, no,' she said, 'you must always be as playful as you have always been, I would not like you to be as grave as some folks I have seen.'" On the 21st of April, Mrs. Livingstone became ill and she died on the 27th, "at the close of a long, clear, hot day, the last Sabbath of April, 1862." She was buried a little to the east of the house where she died and a simple headstone, with an inscription on the one side in

English, on the other side in Portuguese, marks the spot. The grave has become the centre of a small burying ground which is surrounded by a cactus hedge and contains some half dozen graves, mostly Portuguese.

Livingstone was heartbroken, and for the first time in his life he felt himself willing to die. In his book, *The Zambesi and its Tributaries*, he refers to his bereavement with great restraint, and closes with a simple, *"Fiat, Domine, voluntas tua!"* In his private journal and in his letters to his friends he pours out his heart. "I wept over her who well deserved many tears. I loved her when I married her, and the longer I lived with her I. loved her the more. Oh, my Mary, my Mary! how often have we longed for a quiet home, since you and I were cast adrift at Kolobeng. Surely the removal by a kind Father who knoweth our frame means that He rewarded you by taking you to the best home, the eternal one in the heavens." In spite of these crushing sorrows Livingstone heroically continued his work. Sailing up the Shire he proceeded to take his new boat, the *Lady Nyasa,* to pieces, in order to carry it past the Murchison cataracts so that he might launch it on the upper river and steam into the Lake. While thus engaged he received a government despatch from Earl Russell, intimating the recall of the expedition. Even in this moment of disappointment he was keen to do the utmost possible, and before retiring he made a hurried journey westward to the Loangwa valley. Then, rejoining the boat, he led the expedition back to the coast.

VII: *The Slave Trade*

The five years' work on the Zambesi, from 1858 to 1863, had yielded important results in the discovery and opening up of hitherto unknown regions. But the hideous shadow of the slave trade increasingly threw a gloom over all. Livingstone found that the slavers turned his discoveries to their own account. They followed in his track and even represented themselves as "Livingstone's children." The infamous traffic grew to vast dimensions, and populous districts in the interior were being swept bare. Tens of thousands of slaves were annually marched in fetters to the coast, many of whom were murdered in cold blood or left to perish by the way. The soul of Livingstone was moved to its very depths, and he resolved to return to England to fight this fearful traffic to the death and expose the heartless policy of the Portuguese who, while claiming as their own vast countries over which they never had control, were really keeping the ring for the slave raider.

But first he had the *Lady Nyasa* to dispose of. Finding no other plan feasible he boldly sailed her across the Indian Ocean to Bombay, with only fourteen tons of coal in her bunker, and himself acting in the double capacity of captain and engineer. It was perhaps the most foolhardy thing that Livingstone ever did.

From July, 1864, to August, 1865, Livingstone was at home striving to rouse England to an interest in the woes of Africa. The Government maintained a diplomatic reserve in view of the hostility of Portugal, but the nation gained a new knowledge of the nefarious traffic which was bleeding Central Africa to death. Livingstone's eyes were continually turned towards that unhappy region. His own idea of his future work was to return and endeavour to open up the country around the Lakes, from some point on the coast, north of Portuguese territory. The Geographical Society proposed that he should try to determine the position of the watershed of Central Africa. While greatly attracted by this problem, Livingstone replied that he could only feel in the way of duty by working as a missionary. In the end he went out, aided by grants of £500 each from the Government and the Royal Geographical Society, supplemented by £1000 from a private friend. He held the rank of honorary consul without salary, and with a warning to expect no pension! For the rest he must trust to his own resources and his own great heart.

VIII: *Seven Years of Wandering*

He left England, in August, 1865, never to return. At Bombay he sold the *Lady Nyasa,* which had cost him £6000, for £2300, but this sum was soon after entirely lost through the failure of an Indian bank. His friend, Sir Bartle Frere, Governor of Bombay, gave assistance in fitting out the expedition, and commissioned Livingstone to present a steamer to the Sultan of Zanzibar. The Sultan, having received the gift, granted a letter of recommendation to his subjects in the interior. The expedition, when at length it was put ashore in Africa, consisted of a motley assemblage of beasts and men. Six camels, four buffaloes, two mules and four donkeys were brought from India, in the hope that some, if not all of them, would prove immune from the bite of the tsetse fly. From India also came thirteen sepoys and nine Nassick boys, who proved to be worthless. Ten Johanna men were little better. The bright stars of the expedition were two Zambesians, Susi and Chuma, whose devotion has made their names immortal.

It would be impossible to follow Livingstone through the bewildering maze of his seven last years of wandering. The interest of his geographical achievements, great as it is, is eclipsed by the tale of his unparalleled sufferings and deathless heroism. From the first, misfortune seemed to dog his steps. The sepoys and Nassick boys had to be dismissed after they had, by their carelessness and cruelty, killed the beasts of burden. At Lake Nyasa no means of crossing was to be found, and this necessitated a long détour round its southern end. At this point the Johanna men lost heart and deserted. On reaching the coast they related a most circumstantial story that Livingstone had been murdered by the natives and that they had buried him. This story was widely accepted, but Mr. E. D. Young, who knew by experience what liars they were, expressed his disbelief and proved it by a rapid journey up the Shire, where he gathered sufficient information to show that Livingstone was alive and had passed away to the west.

From this point Livingstone's trail on the map bends and doubles and twists about in a seemingly aimless fashion, and raises the question of what was his objective. The answer is supplied by the configuration of the country he was exploring. West of Lake Nyasa, beyond the Loangwa valley, the watershed of Central Africa, now known as the great plateau of North-eastern Rhodesia, runs almost due north and south. On its western side the Congo takes its rise, and begins to crawl like a gigantic snake across the continent. First, under the name of the Chambesi, it flows southward to Lake Bangweolo, creating the impression that it will turn out to be a tributary of the Zambesi. Issuing out of the other end of Lake Bangweolo as the Luapula, it flows directly north to Lake Mweru, passing through which, it continues its northerly course as the Lualaba, and raises a strong presumption that it will prove to be the Nile. Gradually, however, it bends round to the northwest, then to the west, then to the southwest, and finally declares itself at the Atlantic as the Congo. All beautifully plain now upon the map, but in Livingstone's day the undiscovered secret of African waterways, to be painfully searched for through a maze of tropical forests and malarial swamps. Livingstone, with infinite toil and travail, was groping about for the solution of this problem, hoping in his heart of hearts that he might be laying bare the historic fountains of the Nile.

Early in the journey his health broke down and he suffered untold agonies from constantly recurring fever, dysentery and bleeding of the bowels. His feet, too, gave way and became ulcerated. In fact, he had now but the shattered ruins of a once magnificent constitution. Worst of all, one of the carriers bolted with his medicine chest. "I felt," he writes, "as if I had now received the sentence of death." Yet he doggedly plodded on. On the last day of 1866 he writes in his diary, "Will try to do better in 1867, and be better—more gentle and loving, and may the Almighty, to whom I commit my way, bring my desires to pass and prosper me. Let all the sins of '66 be blotted out for Jesus' sake." In 1867 he reached Lake Tanganyika and, striking westward, discovered Lake Mweru. Everywhere he found the ravages of the slave trade, yet he seems to have got on fairly well with some of the traders, and one of them in particular showed him no small kindness.

On New Year's Day, 1868, he writes, "If I am to die this year, prepare me for it." He had now determined to turn back to Ujiji, on the east side of Lake Tanganyika, where he hoped to get letters from home and stores which he had ordered to be sent up from the coast. But first he went south and discovered Lake Bangweolo, then back towards Tanganyika, prostrate with fever and almost at death's door. It is certain he would never have reached Ujiji but for the help of an Arab trader, Mohamad Bogharib, who had him borne along in a litter. Crossing the Lake he reached Ujiji only to find that the stores sent from the coast had almost all disappeared, while of all his letters only one was left. Having written to the coast for fresh supplies, and appealed to the Sultan of Zanzibar for protection against the systematic robbery of his goods, Livingstone resolved, with such resources as he had, to cross Lake Tanganyika and strike northwest to the Manyuema country, in order to determine the course of the Lualaba.

For two years he was lost in the wilds and the world

came to believe that he was dead. His letters never reached the coast. On one occasion forty were dispatched but all were lost. Part of this time was consumed by a long illness, when he was unable to leave his hut for months. There were incessant delays owing to the disturbed state of the country, due to slave raiding. At one time all his men deserted except the faithful Susi and Chuma and another. In his loneliness he found constant solace in his Bible which he read through four times.

It wore on to 1871. "O Father," he writes, "help me to finish this work to Thy glory." In July of this year he was witness of a fearful massacre. The slavers suddenly attacked a native town on market day, shot down hundreds of defenceless people, and drove many more into the river. The story of this dreadful day, when at last it reached England, did more than anything else to rouse the conscience of the nation to a stern resolve that these atrocities must cease.

IX: *Stanley*

Livingstone returned to Ujiji on October 23, 1871, "a mere ruckle of bones," as he says. Again he met with bitter disappointment. The stores he had ordered from the coast and which he so urgently needed, had all been made away with in the belief that he was dead. He found himself destitute and at his wits' end. Five days later help reached him, as suddenly and as providentially as if it had dropped from the sky. On the morning of the 28th Susi rushed in gasping out that he had seen an Englishman. It was H. M. Stanley, a name second only to Livingstone's in the history of African exploration. He had been sent out by the *New York Herald* to find Livingstone dead or alive and bring him home. His appearance was as an angel of mercy, for he came abundantly supplied with stores and medicines. Livingstone revived marvellously in health and spirits. "You have brought me new life," he kept saying. The two men were together for about six months, and explored the north end of Lake Tanganyika. In after years Stanley warmly acknowledged that his life had been profoundly influenced by the Christian nobility of Livingstone's character. He writes enthusiastically, "You may take any point in Dr. Livingstone's character, and I would challenge any man to find a fault in it. . . . His gentleness never forsakes him, his hopefulness never deserts him. No harassing anxieties, distraction of mind, long separation from home and kindred, can make him complain. He thinks 'all will come out right at last,' he has such faith in the goodness of Providence. . . . His is the Spartan heroism, the inflexibility of the Roman, the enduring resolution of the Anglo-Saxon—never to relinquish his work, though his heart yearns for home, never to surrender his obligations until he can write FINIS to his work."

Stanley had found Livingstone, but to bring him home was another matter. He was immovably fixed in his resolve. Accordingly it was agreed that Stanley, on returning to the coast, should send up dependable carriers with whose help Livingstone hoped to finish his task. Till then he refused to go home. Sir Harry Johnston in his biography of Livingstone, after a sustained attempt to represent him as a kind of smoking room hero who had unfortunately stumbled into a missionary career, makes at this point the fatuous suggestion that "posterity can only heave a sigh of vain regret over Livingstone's obstinacy in rejecting Stanley's advice." Among other possible advantages, had Livingstone returned to Europe with Stanley, "he might have lived many years longer, and died a baronet!" Posterity may be trusted to think far other thoughts. Had Livingstone returned, one of the most inspiring chapters of human history would never have been written, and a life of Christlike devotion to downtrodden Africa would not have been crowned by a perfect sacrifice.

Livingstone had five months to wait for the arrival of Stanley's carriers. It was during this time that he wrote a letter to the *New York Herald,* in which occur the famous words, now carved on his tomb in Westminster, "All I can add in my loneliness is, may Heaven's rich blessing come down on every one—American, English or Turk—who will help to heal the open sore of the world." On the 14th of August, 1872, the carriers arrived and proved thoroughly satisfactory. "I have a party of good men, selected by H. M. Stanley. A dutiful son could not have done more than he generously did. I bless him. The men, fifty-six in number, have behaved as well as the Makololo. I cannot award them higher praise." Among them was Jacob Wainwright, an educated Nassick boy, whose services at Livingstone's death and afterwards rank his name with those of Susi and Chuma.

X: *The Long Last Mile*

On the 25th of August Livingstone set out on his last journey. His plan was to circle round the south end of Lake Bangweolo, in order to make sure of taking in all the sources of the river, and then to follow its course northwards. Having settled the question of whether it was the Nile or the Congo, he would then come home. Not to rest, however, but to expose the enormities of the slave trade, for this, more than the geographical problem, was his supreme interest. "If the good Lord permits me to put a stop to the enormous evils of the inland slave-trade, I shall not grudge my hunger and toils. The Nile sources are valuable to me only as a means of enabling me to open my mouth with power among men." It was not given him to carry out his plan. The main end he had in view was indeed attained, not by discovery as he had hoped, but far more effectually by the sacrifice of his life. He was one of those chosen ones to whom it is given, like God's own Son, to help the world most of all by their dying.

Livingstone's strength was no longer equal to the task he had set himself. First baked by the intense heat, and then, after the rainy season came, drenched day after day, his health broke down completely. By the end of the year he had reached the neighbourhood of Lake Bangweolo. All the grassy flats for miles around the Lake were waterlogged, and among these interminable sponges Livingstone's party floundered for weeks. At last, too weak to walk, he was carried on the men's shoulders, and then in a rudely constructed *machila.* He notes, "this trip has made my hair all grey." It was the desperate struggle of a dying man, gifted with the most indomitable spirit that ever housed in mortal clay. On the 19th of March, his last birthday, he writes, "Thanks to the Almighty Preserver of men for sparing me thus far on the journey of life. Can I hope for ultimate success? So many obstacles have arisen. Let not Satan prevail over me, O my good Lord Jesus." A few days later he was crouching for shelter under an upturned canoe, miserably cold and wet, his tent torn with the wind and soaked. Then it was that he wrote the words, "Nothing earthly will make me give up my work in despair. I encourage myself in the Lord my God and go forward."

Gradually he became too weak even to be carried. The last entry in his journal stands under the date, April 27, "Knocked up quite and remain—recover— sent to buy milch goats. We are on the banks of R. Molilamo." Two days later he was moved a short distance to Chitambo's village where a hut was hastily built for him. Towards evening his mind wandered, but about midnight Susi brought him some hot water and he was able with great difficulty to mix some medicine for himself. Then he said faintly, "All right, you can go now." When the boy who slept in the hut with him awoke about four o'clock in the morning he found his master dead on his knees at the bedside. It was the 1st (or perhaps more probably the 4th) of May, 1873.

XI: *Home*

His faithful men resolved that his body, at whatever cost, must be carried home to his own people, and they prepared for this extraordinary task with the greatest care and thoroughness. An exact inventory was made by Jacob Wainwright of all his possessions. The body was dried and rudely embalmed. The heart was buried under a tree upon which his name was carved. This sacred spot is now marked by an obelisk in the middle of a square clearing in the forest, and is held in trust by the United Free Church of Scotland, which has a mission station at Chitambo, as near to the grave as conditions of health will permit.

Having prepared the body for the journey the men set out for the coast, which they reached after nine months of toilsome and perilous marching. When well on the way they met an expedition coming up country to the relief of Livingstone. These Englishmen advised them to go no farther, but to bury the body where they were. They also rummaged through Livingstone's boxes and appropriated some things to their own use. So gross were their perceptions, so blind were they to the moral sublimity of what these sons of Africa were doing!

Livingstone's men held on their way and on February 15, 1874, reached the coast opposite Zanzibar, where they delivered his body to the British consul. It was brought home to England, and after being identified by the old fracture in the arm it was finally laid to rest in the nave of Westminster Abbey, on Saturday, April 18, 1874.

The impression made by the death of Livingstone upon the mind of the civilised world was profound, and it would be impossible to overestimate his influence on the development of Africa. He had travelled thirty thousand miles through the heart of the Dark Continent, and wherever he passed he left a trail of light. He sounded the death knell of the slave trade and opened the country for legitimate commerce. His death marked a new era in Christian missions. But his greatest gift to the world was just to have been himself. Born in a commercial age he brought back to earth the spirit of old romance, and his name will shine for ever with the radiance of saint, of knight-errant, and of martyr.

CHAPTER IV

JOHN MACKENZIE, MISSIONARY STATESMAN

I: *The Elgin Apprentice*

In the ancient ruins of Elgin Cathedral there is pointed out a rude stone trough, possibly a baptismal font, where it is said a poor mother was wont to lay her baby when she went out to work. That baby became General Anderson, who founded and endowed the Anderson Institute, "for the support of old age and the education of youth." In 1845 a little lad of nine was admitted to the Institution, having walked sixteen miles from his native parish of Knockando. His name was John Mackenzie, and he was destined to become famous as an African missionary and statesman. He was the son of a crofter on Speyside, the youngest of six children, and was born on August 30, 1835. The bare soil of the upland croft provided but a scanty living for the family, so his parents thankfully accepted the opportunity of placing their youngest boy in the Anderson Institution. Thus commenced his connection with Elgin, which became the home of his boyhood and youth.

On leaving the Institution in his fourteenth year Mackenzie was apprenticed to Mr. Russell, the printer and publisher of the *Elgin Courant*. Here he worked on an average ten hours a day with a good deal of overtime. His leisure, such as it was, was entirely at his own disposal, for he lived alone in lodgings and was his own master. How singularly independent his boyhood was, is brought out by an entry in his diary, made in his twentieth year. "It is now ten years since I have asked parental advice. During that period, when not under the eye of a teacher or of an employer, I have been entirely my own adviser, and my own master. Instead of giving, both parents ask advice from me." The summer evenings were devoted to cricket; in the winter the Bishopmill Literary Association stimulated interests of another sort.

When about eighteen years of age Mackenzie came under the influence of Alexander Williamson, afterwards a well known missionary in China, who in the summer of 1853 conducted the services in the Independent Chapel at Elgin. From this time he dated both his conversion and his desire to be a missionary. That desire burned very intensely within him, and he prayed earnestly for some door to open that would give him release from his long apprenticeship. His whole religious life at this period, as revealed in his private diary, bears the marks of extreme spiritual tension. Thus he writes in 1854, *"Sept. 9th. The war is going on incessantly, only God is gracious and upholds me. I have an increasing desire to work for God, and I am only happy at present in the office from the prospect of soon leaving it." "Sept. 17th, Sunday. At the communion table today I felt more overcome than ever before. What a glorious feeling! Dear Jesus! He was not there hidden as He often is to my darkened mind. Heaven seemed very near, life very* short, and to spend my life as a missionary of the Gospel appeared a glorious work indeed. Oh, I felt eager to engage in it! Surely God, when he thinks proper, will open a door for me." "*Sept. 19th.* Felt some strange doubts sweep into my mind this afternoon. . . . They strike at the very root. . . . God help this darkened, blinded, stumbling, but trusting and confiding soul! For Jesus' sake!" No doubt it was out of these struggles and prayers that there emerged the Mackenzie of later years, strong, calm and patient almost beyond belief.

During the ensuing winter his health showed some alarming symptoms, which led to his release from his apprenticeship and his return to his home in Knockando. Believing that this was likely to be his final parting from Elgin, he delivered a farewell address to his old companions in the town from the pulpit of the Independent Chapel. The intense passion of the youthful preacher, unduly excited perhaps by the occasion and by the sight of the crowded audience of young men, made a deep and lasting impression.

II: *The Resolved Man*

In September, 1855, Mackenzie was accepted for training by the London Missionary Society. A previous application had been declined on the ground of his youth and inexperience, but now the way was open for the attaining of his heart's desire. He was sent to Bedford to study for two years under the Rev. J. Jukes, the Congregational minister there. Subsequently he went for a session to Edinburgh, where he continued his studies in theology and also in medicine. He was a hard working student and exceedingly rigorous in the demands he made upon himself. Thus he writes in his diary, "Oh, if I strained every nerve for Christ! I must do this. I will do it in the strength of the Lord. Have obtained much consolation and strength and encouragement from the thought that the Lord will help the *resolved* man. . . . I have now a set of resolutions for the guidance of my life drawn up, which I read on my knees three times a day. . . . I have resolved to live to Christ and to live for Christ. I must conquer every evil habit, *that's settled*. Idleness, irresolution, carelessness, timidity, irregularity, all must be swept away. In the strength of the living God, the Helper of the aspirant, I will set to work. . . . We have not enough of devoted *personal* attachment to Him whom we call our Saviour. Oh, let us be extreme on this point, let us burn with love, and yearn earnestly to testify in actions the existence of this love."

Under this high pressure his health gave way. In his morbid conscientiousness he had been half starving himself, so that though now nearly six feet in height, he weighed only eight stone. He became oppressed with a gloomy foreboding that his life would be an utter failure. Out of this Slough of Despond he was delivered by the wise counsel of a London doctor, who told him the truth about his condition. At once Mackenzie's strong sense asserted itself, and henceforth he led a saner and healthier, though none the less ardent, Christian life.

On the 19th of April, 1858, Mackenzie was ordained in the Queen Street Hall, Edinburgh, for service in

South Africa. Shortly afterwards he was married to Helen Douglas of Portobello, the sister of a college friend, whose devoted love sustained him through all the long years of labour and warfare that fell to his lot. The young couple sailed on June 5 and reached Cape Town July 14. A description of Mackenzie's personal appearance, though written somewhat later, may not inappropriately be given here. "A tall, square-built man, about five feet eleven inches in height, fair in complexion, genial in countenance, with great strength of character stamped on his brow, and an unmistakable Highlander, speaking the English language with wonderful purity and intonation."

III : *Following up Livingstone*

His arrival in Africa occurred at a moment of considerable interest in the history of African missions. Livingstone's great journey had roused the home country and he was now going out as British consul to take up his work of exploration on the Zambesi. His challenge to the Churches had met with a warm response, and the London Missionary Society resolved to plant missions among the Matabele and the Makololo. Sekeletu, the Makololo chief, who lived with his tribe among the swamps of the upper Zambesi, was understood to have expressed to Livingstone his willingness to move to a healthier region farther east. This would no doubt expose him to attack from the Matabele across the river, but it was hoped that the influence of the two missions would be sufficient to keep the peace and reconcile these warlike tribes. It was a bold and well-conceived scheme, the one which promised, if successful, to lead to the most important results in the Christian development of Central Africa.

Three young missionaries with their wives sailed in the company of the Mackenzies to Cape Town. Of these, Messrs. Sykes and Thomas were destined for the Matabele, while Mr. Price was to be Mackenzie's colleague to the Makololo. Dr. Moffat was to superintend the planting of the Matabele mission; Mr. Helmore, an African missionary of experience, was put in charge of the expedition to the Makololo. The mission party travelled north from the Cape, and after much difficulty through the death of many of their oxen they at length reached Dr. Moffat's station of Kuruman. Here they had their first pleasing impressions of what mission work could do for the natives. When the Sabbath bell rang out its summons groups of decently dressed people were to be seen wending their way to church, many of them carrying their Sechuana Bibles and hymn books. Evidences were not wanting of industrial progress, in the better cultivation of the land and the use of improved implements. Indeed, there were Bechuana farmers who had reached a standard of civilisation at least equal to that of the Boers across the border in the Transvaal.

IV: *The Makololo Disaster*

Preparations were at once begun for launching the Makololo mission. In view of the difficulties likely to be encountered in crossing the Kalahari Desert and the swamps of the Zambesi, Mackenzie proposed that the missionaries should leave their wives behind at Kuruman till they had secured the removal of Sekeletu's tribe to a healthier region and established the mission station. This plan was decisively rejected by Mr. Helmore whose wife was determined to accompany her husband with her four children. In view of the tragedy that followed and the criticism aroused, it is only fair to remember that Livingstone had taken his wife and children with him on his first visit to the Makololo. It was natural, therefore, as Mackenzie says, that other missionaries' wives should "venture to hope that they could go where Mrs. Livingstone had been, and reside where their husbands resided."

Finally it was arranged that Mr. and Mrs. Price and their baby should accompany the Helmores, and that the Mackenzies should follow the next year with supplies. The pioneer party set out and, after a terrible struggle, crossed the Kalahari Desert. The sufferings of the children must have been dreadful. Livingstone has described his feelings under the same conditions when he saw his children like to die of thirst before his eyes. Mrs. Helmore's letters tell a pitiful story. "Tuesday the 6th was one of the most trying days I ever passed. We were all faint with thirst, and of course eating was out of the question. The poor children continually asked for water. I put them off as long as I could, and when they could be denied no longer, doled the precious fluid out a spoonful at a time. Poor Selina and Henry cried bitterly. Willie bore up manfully but his sunken eyes showed how much he suffered. As for dear Lizzie she did not utter a word of complaint, nor even asked for water, but lay all the day on the ground perfectly quiet, her lips quite parched and blackened."

Next season, in May, 1860, the Mackenzies started on their long trek to the north. They passed the ruins of Kolobeng, Livingstone's station which had been destroyed by the Boers. As Theal, the South African historian has suggested that Livingstone's house was looted by the natives, it may be mentioned that Mackenzie afterwards became acquainted with Boers who had articles of Livingstone's furniture in their houses, and who did not deny the raid. Still farther north they came to Shoshong, the town of the Bamangwato, which in after years became their home. Here they met Dr. Moffat returning from the Matabele where the new mission had been successfully established. No news had as yet come through from Helmore and his party.

Mackenzie now pushed out into "the great thirst land," where he was entirely dependent on the guidance of the Bushmen. Here a rumour reached him of disaster having befallen his friends, but he disregarded it and continued to advance. The Bushmen, however, by a kindly deception led him westward till they brought him to the Zouga river near Lake Ngami. Here he met a party of natives who said that a white man and two children were with their chief, higher up the river. Mackenzie had some reason to suspect the truth of this story, for the chief in question was an enemy of the Makololo, and wished to prevent missionaries reaching them. He therefore resolved still to go on, but he had not proceeded far when he met Mr. Price, who, ill and half distracted with his sufferings, had been brought down the river. In broken accents his tragic tale was told. His wife and child were dead, also Mr. and Mrs. Helmore and two of their children. Sekeletu had treated them with great callousness, and was even suspected of having poisoned them. When they sickened and died in rapid succession he claimed all their property, and when Mr. Price left with the two surviving children the guides led them through a belt of tsetse fly, so that all the oxen died. Thus it was that Mackenzie found them stranded and destitute on the Zouga.

The injustice and cruelty of Sekeletu, so different from his magnificent help of Livingstone, may perhaps be best accounted for by the fact that he was in reality a weakling. On this occasion he fell under the influence of a renegade member of the missionary party, who counselled him to make away with the white men and seize their goods. Afterwards he expressed contrition when he found his conduct reprobated through all the tribes, as an unparalleled breach of hospitality to men whom he had himself invited to his country.

Not long after this the story of the Makololo came to a dark and bloody end. Their vassals, the Barotsi, planned a sudden rising and put them to death in a single night, an African St. Bartholomew. A fugitive party escaped and reached the Zouga, only to be massacred by the tribe that had sheltered Mr. Price. Thus perished the Makololo. "I do not venture," says Mackenzie, "to affirm the presence of divine retribution in this tragic end of the Makololo. But in Bechuanaland, and especially among the heathen in the northern part, the feeling is very general that the destruction of the Makololo, so soon after their inhospitable and perfidious conduct towards the missionaries, is to be traced to the vengeance of God. Nor is this mere theory in the native mind, for in some of our difficulties at Shoshong, when sinister counsels had almost prevailed, some Gamaliel was sure to stand up and advise, 'Let the missionary alone. The Makololo injured the missionaries, and where are the Makololo?' "

The disaster to the mission party was a deep personal grief to the Mackenzies and a heavy blow to their hopes. It was a sad company that struggled back through the desert. The children behaved like heroes. Mackenzie tells how he was touched by a conversation he overheard between them. Little Willie remarked to his sister that he was very thirsty. Was the water all gone? His sister, who was older than he, answered that "he must be a good boy, and not ask for water. Did he not remember how they had been thirsty long ago, when mamma was still living? They must not ask for water." The water happened to be plentiful and Mackenzie had the pleasure of giving the little fellow a hearty drink. Kuruman was reached in February, 1861, after an absence of nine months, and the orphan children were sent home to England.

V: *In Khama's Country*

For some time the Directors of the London Missionary Society were in doubt as to policy, and in the meantime Mackenzie was sent to begin work in Shoshong. Here he would be in position to keep in touch with the Zambesi, and if a favourable opportunity arose, to make a fresh attempt to establish the Makololo mission. The massacre of that tribe, however, put an end to these hopes, and Mackenzie settled down to permanent work in Shoshong. The town numbered about 30,000 inhabitants. It lay under a ridge of rocky hills which provided a refuge in time of war. Sekhome, the chief, was an unscrupulous schemer, but his son Khama was a young man of great promise, who afterwards became known as a high-principled Christian ruler, one of the noblest that Africa has produced. The influence which Mackenzie had in forming his character and shaping his policy was one of his finest services to Bechuanaland.

In 1862 the dreaded Matabele made an attack on Shoshong. The women and children took refuge in the mountain, and with them went Mrs. Mackenzie and her children, for it was known that the Matabele, when on the warpath, spared neither sex nor age. Sekhome, as high priest of the tribe, began his incantations, but Khama cut him short, and leading out some of the younger regiments repelled the enemy. During the crisis Mackenzie had preached on the Christian attitude to war and the duty of defending one's home. This, with the courage of Khama, gave the heathen chiefs and people a new view of things. "We were told," they said, "that when a man became a Christian he was bound not to fight in any cause. We therefore expected that all the 'men of the word of God' would have ascended the mountain with the women and children. But to-day those who pray to God are our leaders."

Next year Mackenzie was sent to reinforce the Matabele mission in the absence of some of his colleagues. At first Mosilikatse refused him permission to enter Matabeleland because he was Sekhome's missionary but this objection was overcome, and in the end the chief offered him a site for a mission station if he would reside permanently in the country. During this visit Mackenzie gained an intimate knowledge of the savage military system of the Matabele, a system which broke up home life and made progress impossible. Hordes of young warriors, herded together in barracks, and living only for bloodshed and plunder, were a source of disquiet and terror to the tribes far and near. Missionaries were admitted to the country but the people were forbiden to learn. More and more it was becoming apparent that this military empire must change or one day be shattered.

Returning to Shoshong in 1864 Mackenzie settled down feeling that here was to be the scene of his life work, and such it proved to be for the next twelve years. The Gospel had first been preached in Shoshong by Livingstone when travelling to Lake Ngami. A native teacher had continued the work, and for some time a Lutheran missionary had laboured in the town. When Mackenzie arrived there was the nucleus of a Christian church, enrolled, as he thought, prematurely. It was his task to instruct those who were already favourable to the Gospel and to evangelise the mass of the people who were still heathen. In order to reach them he preached at various public places through the town. When the little band of ill-taught converts painfully attempted to sing a hymn the heathens were vastly amused. "What are they doing?"

was asked. "They are raising the death cry," suggested some wag, and the phrase stuck. In conducting school Mackenzie found much encouragement in the progress of his pupils. "I came to the conclusion," he says, "that the mental ability of those I was teaching was probably as great as in a village school in a country district in England." The missionary's home life was something new and wonderful to the native mind. "After being shown, at their own request, some of the rooms of our house, a party of the wives of petty chiefs at length broke out, addressing Mrs. Mackenzie, 'Happy wife and happy mother! You have a kingdom here of your own'!"

Sekhome, the chief, showed for a time some interest in the new doctrine. "I found," writes Mackenzie, "that this man with the sinister face, who was the greatest sorcerer in Bechuanaland, who was hated by many and mistrusted by all his neighbours, had a keen appreciation of the character and the object of the Gospel of Jesus Christ. 'It is all very good for you white men to follow the Word of God,' he would say. 'God made you with straight hearts like this,'—holding out his finger straight—'but it is a different thing for us black people. God made us with a crooked heart like this,'—holding out his bent finger. When assured that both black and white needed and could receive a new and right heart, 'Not black people,' he said, 'and yet, after all, Khama's heart is perhaps right. Yes, Khama's heart is right.'" When pressed to follow his son's example he seemed to regard it as impossible. "When I think of entering the Word of

God," he said, "it is like going out into the plain and meeting all the forces of the Matabele single-handed."

When Sekhome rejected the Gospel it was but a short step for him to become a persecutor. He ordered his son to marry another wife and conform to heathen customs. When Khama refused he ordered him to be put to death, but found that he was too popular to be thus dealt with. There followed a period of plotting and of civil war, during which Khama behaved with extraordinary restraint and Christian consistency. Several times his father was completely in his power, but, like David with King Saul, he refused to avenge himself. In the end Sekhome found himself a fugitive from his tribe, and his brother Macheng, who had long been a prisoner among the Matabele, was restored to the chieftainship.

These events greatly disturbed the work of the mission, but Mackenzie held fearlessly on his way. It is typical of his straightforward courage and of the influence he had won, that when Khama and his followers were driven to the mountain, he went to Sekhome and obtained permission to visit them and conduct services every Sunday. On the other hand, when Sekhome himself had to flee, after the failure of a plot to assassinate his brother and son, it was in Mackenzie's house that he sought refuge ere he escaped under cover of darkness. Macheng, the new chief, though himself a heathen, declared, "Since I arrived at Shoshong I have seen and heard for myself. The people of the Word of God alone speak the truth."

In 1867 gold was discovered on the Tati River, in the district lying between Shoshong and the Matabele country, and immediately greedy eyes were turned thither. The Boers tried to stir up a native war, and officially expressed the pious hope of seeing "the vagabonds at Shoshong set on fire." Mackenzie was thus brought face to face with a problem he had long brooded upon, and which was to become paramount in his life,—the problem of the development of South Africa and the safeguarding of the native races. On this occasion the chief Macheng, acting on Mackenzie's advice, petitioned the British Government to take him and his people under their protection before the rush of gold diggers and land grabbers should begin.

In the same year a church was built at Shoshong, and Mackenzie has given a vivid and amusing picture of the scene on the opening day. "Early on Tuesday the people began to assemble. Each division of the town came headed by its chief. Heathen men with hoary heads, toothless and tottering with old age, came leaning on their staffs. Full grown men—the haughty, the cunning, the fierce—came, with those younger in years, of brighter eye and more hopeful mien. We had the usual members of the congregation, some of whom were neatly dressed. But sticklers for the proprieties would have been shocked to see a man moving in the crowd who considered himself well dressed though wearing a shirt only, another with trousers only, a third with a black 'swallow-tail,' closely buttoned to the chin—the only piece of European clothing which the man wore—another with a soldier's red coat, overshadowed by an immense wide-awake hat. . . . The church doors were thrown open and many strange remarks were made with reference to the building.

One man said, 'What a splendid place to drink beer in!' another, 'What a capital pen for sheep and goats!' and a third declared that with a few people inside they could defy the Matabele nation." For the feast an ox was killed and prepared, with a plentiful supply of sour milk and tea. Near the end of the feast it was found that a certain head man had been overlooked. The meat was all gone, and the milk, but the chief was equal to the occasion. Handing the man a large kettle of tea he said tactfully, "Drink, for there is no longer aught to eat. The tea was prepared at the same fire as the meat, it is therefore quite the same thing. Drink, for tea is your part of the feast." The man quietly sat down with his kettle of tea and drank it all.

The year 1870 was spent at home on furlough, when, besides doing the usual deputation work, Mackenzie wrote his book, *Ten Years North of the Orange River,* in which he gives a remarkably clear and interesting account of tribal life and mission work in South Africa. Returning to Shoshong in 1871 he continued his work there for five years. The church prospered and Khama continued to grow in wisdom and Christian character. On becoming chief he substituted a Christian service for the heathen ceremonies that were customary in connection with the sowing of the seed. He also made a law that white traders were not to bring strong drink into his country. The number of traders and hunters who came to Shoshong was increasing year by year, and it was Mackenzie's habit to hold a service for them in his house every Sunday afternoon. Captain Parker Gilmore, in his book, *The*

Great Thirst Land, describes one such service. "Sunday came round, and I could have known the day from all others by the air of rest that lay over Shoshong. . . . In the little parlour, where worship was held, the presence of the Almighty might almost be felt. In my early life I had regarded religion lightly, but when I looked upon half a dozen stalwart men accustomed to everyday hardship and danger, our worthy pastor's children and a few servants, giving their whole soul to what they were engaged in, I more forcibly felt than ever I did before that there was a great God above us, One who invited our adoration and love. . . . That was the most solemn Sunday I ever passed."

VI: *When Black Meets White*

In 1876 Mackenzie was moved to Kuruman to take charge of the Moffat Institution which was being built there. This Institution, for the training of native pastors and teachers, was a memorial to Dr. Moffat, and, owing to the great liberality of subscribers, the Directors of the London Missionary Society proceeded to plan the work on a larger scale than was considered prudent by the missionaries on the spot. Mackenzie, therefore, besides his work of teaching and preaching, was saddled with the task of erecting buildings worth £10,000. This he did in such a manner as to call forth the warmest praise of the Government inspector of works.

From this point Mackenzie began to find himself drawn irresistibly into the wide and turbid stream of South African and Imperial politics. This arose out of work which came to him in the way of duty, work to be done for the defence of those African tribes to whom he had consecrated his life. Many of the natives had made considerable progress in agriculture, but now cases occurred in which white men stepped in and seized their farms. Even when appeal was made to the nearest court in the Colony, the intruders sat tight and defied the law. These occurrences gave rise to a miserable state of turmoil and unrest, which at last broke out in open rebellion. The white settlers in the neighbourhood of Kuruman took refuge in the Institution. Mackenzie refused to ask Government protection for the mission, as he did not consider it to be the duty of the Government to safeguard missionaries working among heathen tribes, but he left others free to act as they judged best. How little he feared the rebels may be gathered from the fact that he walked alone to their camp to secure the safety of some men who were coming from Kimberley. He long afterwards remembered vividly that on this adventure he saw, what he had recognised on one or two occasions at Shoshong, the passionate lust for blood looking at him greedily from the eyes of native men. It was indeed a bolder venture than the much vaunted deed of Cecil Rhodes who visited the Matabele camp only after they were broken and cowed and desirous of peace. Not without reason did Mackenzie enjoy among the natives the surname of *Tau*, the lion.

During the quelling of the rebellion he had much correspondence with the authorities, in which he urged upon them the moral obligation resting on Britain to maintain law and order in Bechuanaland, and to secure to the progressive native farmers the peaceful possession of their farms. This he knew to be the unanimous desire of the chiefs and of the tribesmen. Britain, however, withdrew and, while claiming nominal sovereignty, failed to provide real government. The deplorable result was that bands of Boer raiders crossed the border and seized two districts, which they named Stellaland and Goshen.

VII: *The Battle for Bechuanaland*

In 1882 Mackenzie left for his second furlough, resolved to fight with his whole strength the battle for Bechuanaland. The forces arrayed against him were extremely formidable,—the powerful influence of land-grabbers who cared nothing for native rights and who found their profit in fishing in troubled waters, the territorial ambition of the Boers who were determined to annex Bechuanaland and close the road to the north, above all the ignorance and indifference of Britain. Many at home were frankly callous as to the fate of the natives, believing that they were doomed to extinction like the American Indians. A prominent member of the Government said they would "go as the Choctaws had done." "It went to my heart like a knell," was Mackenzie's comment. Others were conscientiously opposed to any advance which would increase the already vast responsibilities of the Empire. The nation generally was in total ignorance of the real situation. Mackenzie had to convince the people of England that the question was not whether the native tribes should be left alone,—already the tide of immigration was pouring over them and could not be stayed, —but whether a firm Government was to be interposed between them and the rapacity of unjust and cruel men. "The real question was," he wrote, "were they to go north with the stain of human blood on their hands, or were they to go north as Christians, clean-handed?" He commenced a vigorous campaign, and by speeches, articles, letters and personal interviews he gradually impressed his ideas upon the public mind.

In 1883 a deputation from the Transvaal headed by Kruger, came to London to press for various concessions, including the annexation of all Bechuanaland. The paramount chief of the Bechuanas set out for England to defend his country, but finding himself unable to get beyond Cape Town, he appointed Mackenzie to represent him. "I belong to the Queen," he wrote. "Plead for me! Help me! If the Government does not help me I am destroyed." Mackenzie needed no spur. With great skill and determination he fought the pretensions of the Boers, and defeated their projection of annexation. In the end Britain assumed the protectorate of Bechuanaland, and Mackenzie was appointed the first Deputy-Commissioner. This office he undertook with the cordial approval of the London Missionary Society.

It would be impossible within our limits to follow Mackenzie through all the tangled maze of political intrigue into which he was now plunged. Arriving at the Cape in 1884 he travelled north to Bechuanaland without any military force, and succeeded in conciliating all but an extreme minority of the Stellalanders. But his policy of justice to the natives roused the fierce hostility of all the land-grabbing and gold-mining interests, to whom the native was but a pawn in the white man's game. The whole Boer influence was against him. He now also crossed the path of the great but unscrupulous Cecil Rhodes, whose dreams were more befitting a Roman Emperor than a Christian statesman. Mackenzie was therefore assailed and maligned with extreme bitterness. Part of the secret of this enmity was revealed with cynical frankness in a letter which afterwards came to light, in which he was referred to as "a political suicide, that is to say, an honest man who is not to be bought."

Weary of it all Mackenzie sighs, "If one had only fair play," a wish as reasonable as it was futile. Rhodes by a disgraceful intrigue secured Mackenzie's recall and his own appointment as Commissioner. This, however, did not improve matters, and in 1885 Sir Charles Warren was sent out at the head of a strong expedition to settle Bechuanaland. Entering on his task he began to unravel a discreditable tangle. He found that important despatches had been suppressed, and in particular a petition in favour of Mackenzie signed by the majority of the Stellalanders. This petition Cecil Rhodes had in his pocket while he continued to assure the Government that Mackenzie's policy had excited universal hostility. Thereupon Sir Charles Warren, having expressed his mind freely to Rhodes, made Mackenzie his right hand man during his stay in Bechuanaland. At the close of the expedition he referred to his work in the highest terms. "I cannot too strongly express how much I am indebted to him for the assistance he has rendered to Her Majesty's Government. . . . The confidence reposed in him by not only the native tribes but also by the Dutch and English population has been most marked, and I consider the complete success of the expedition is due in a marked degree to his cordial co-operation and aid. . . . I am convinced that if Mr. Mackenzie had had fair play he would have settled these territories at the time he came up without a stronger force than two hundred police."

When the Warren expedition was withdrawn it was soon apparent that Bechuanaland was in danger of relapsing to the old conditions of disorder. To prevent, if possible, this frustration of hope, Mackenzie returned to England and resumed his work of educating public opinion. To aid in this he wrote his book, *Austral Africa,* in which he set forth with much impressiveness his conception of Britain's mission as a Christian and civilizing power in South Africa. "I know of nothing," he wrote, "which illustrates the present South African position so well as the condition of the United States of America before the civil war. The great question then was, Shall the new territories become Free Soil or Slave States?" Believing then that a great moral issue was at stake, he fought on. But powerful influences of another sort were at work. Through the genius and force of Cecil Rhodes the British South Africa Company was founded with almost unlimited means at its disposal, and it received from the Government a charter for the development of the vast territories now known as Rhodesia. This, though securing these regions for British influence, was far from fulfilling Mackenzie's ideal, and he lived to condemn with no uncertain voice the Company's treatment of the natives. It illustrates his magnanimity that, on reading that the British South Africa pioneers proposed to travel by a route which would inevitably bring them into conflict with the Matabele, he wrote a warning to the Company, giving a sketch and full details of a safer route, which was accordingly adopted. Though his highest hopes had been disappointed he had at least secured the Protectorate of Bechuanaland, and a proposal was at one time favourably considered of reappointing him Commissioner. When this fell through he felt himself free to return to his work as a missionary.

VIII: *"Among God's Little Ones, Content"*

During the years of conflict his connection with the London Missionary Society had been closely maintained, for it was recognised that he was fighting the battle of the mission as well as of the native. When he was retired from his commissionership the Directors cabled to him to resume his salary as a married missionary. This act gave him as much pure pleasure as any event of his public life. "Now, what do you think," he wrote, "of the dear old L.M.S.? I mean to say it is nobly done. I count it one of the honours of my life to reconnect myself in this way. I shall accept the honour but I trust I shall not need to draw the money. I feel quite lifted up with great thankfulness that the Directors are such broad-minded, thoughtful, Christian gentlemen."

It was not considered expedient that Mackenzie

should return to the Bechuanas.   Accordingly he was appointed to take charge of the mission station of Hankey, a settlement about fifty miles from Port Elizabeth.   Here he spent the last seven years of his life.   It was a great change for one who had been for years a leading figure in the national life, to be set to work in this quiet corner, but it was work that brought restfulness and peace of heart.   The situation at Hankey was peculiar, and such as called for those qualities of firmness and patience, good sense and statesmanship which had been exercised in a wider field.   The mission station had an estate of over 4000 acres attached to it.   The original intention had been to settle native converts upon it, but this policy, proving unsuitable, was abandoned and permission obtained from the Colonial Government to sell the land to the native tenants.   This had not been carried out, rents were in arrears, irrigation had been neglected, and things generally were in a mess.   Mackenzie's task, in addition to the ordinary work of a missionary, was "to put Hankey right from top to bottom."   With characteristic energy he set himself to learn High Dutch, in which language he had now to preach.   Before leaving England he had bought the necessary books and, aided by his previous knowledge of the South African *Taal,* he was able on the first Sunday after his arrival at Hankey to conduct the whole service and preach the sermon in Dutch.

Intent on his work he shut himself up in the little valley of Hankey, even refusing for many weeks to read the newspapers or take any part in public life until he had mastered the problem before him.   It was a complex one, including questions of land tenure, irrigation, roadmaking, etc., besides school and church work. Gradually order began to appear out of chaos. One who watched his work wrote of him, "He can wait, and if you cannot do that here, you are not good for much. The things he has had to stand, the bickerings, trials, small intrigues, and insults, are incredible. They would have sent any other man mad in a month. . . . And what has come of it all? Why, the place is changed." It was the same spirit of Christian patience as he had displayed in negotiating with the Stella-landers, when a Government official burst from the room saying, "He must be more than human to stand what he does."

As a preacher he was at his best on communion Sundays. Then his manner became peculiarly tender and his voice thrilled with emotion. As time passed he had the joy of seeing of the fruit of his labours in a considerable increase of the native church, and in a quickening of religious life among the white settlers. In his own character his friends noted a singular ripening and mellowing. His only brother and his four sisters all died in rapid succession in Scotland, leaving him the sole survivor of his family. Writing about this time to one who had been bereaved he says, "Do not lose heart in your loneliness—grasp the pilgrim staff more firmly. Each of us must work out his day resolutely and with his very best efforts." "Resolutely" —he is still of the mind that "the Lord will help the resolved man."

In his last years he took little part in public life, beyond contributing articles to the leading English reviews when asked to do so. Events occurred which caused him deep and anxious sorrow, such as the Jameson raid, the war in South Bechuanaland, and some of the doings of the Chartered Company in Rhodesia. Yet his mind was singularly free from bitterness. On reading in a newspaper a reference to "Mackenzie and Rhodes" as great enemies, he was much distressed and, turning to his wife, said with deep feeling that there was no one beyond his own family for whom he prayed more constantly than Cecil Rhodes. In 1895 his old friend Khama with two other Bechuana chiefs came to England to protest against the Chartered Company's attempt to annex their country. No African perhaps ever made a more favourable impression on the British public than did Khama. His progress through England and Scotland was a triumph and his mission a complete success. This was naturally a great delight to Mackenzie, and probably it is as Khama's missionary that he will longest be remembered by many.

The arduous labours of his life now began to tell upon him increasingly. Several years before, in the midst of his public anxieties, he had a sudden seizure when conducting a service at Berwick-on-Tweed. In October, 1898, another stroke fell upon him, and though he made a partial recovery and was able to go on a visit to his son in Kimberley, he again had an attack and died on March 23rd, 1899, in his 64th year.

Mackenzie's career is a powerful reminder of the vast forces, political, industrial and social, against which the Christian missionary in Africa has to struggle, forces that embitter race feeling and hinder the advance of the Gospel. He was a farseeing man, a great Christian statesman and a true imperialist. To him belongs the honour of having been the man who first forced Britain to face her God-given task of controlling the destinies of the entire region from the Cape to the Zambesi. His policy did not find immediate acceptance, for a prophet has often as little honour in his own generation as in his own country, but it is the same ideal which has led to the policy of Mandates, now taking shape under the auspices of the League of Nations. The native problem in South Africa is by no means solved, but still causes the gravest anxiety to responsible statesmen. Only the future can reveal whether the ignorant tyranny of the Boers, the flagrant injustice of the land-grabbers and the selfish imperialism of Cecil Rhodes may not have laid up, deep in the mind of the African, a store of resentment which may yet have to be dearly paid for. Certain it is that if such a dire result is to be averted it will only be by the patient and steady application of those principles of Christian justice and brotherhood which Mackenzie so powerfully advocated, to heal the wounds already made.

CHAPTER V

When David Livingstone, after crossing the African continent, appealed to the Christians of Britain to enter by the door which he had opened, there was a young student in Scotland who felt this as a personal call, and resolved to give his life to the redemption of Central Africa. In the providence of God he found his work in South, rather than Central, Africa, but his pioneering on the Zambesi, and the impulse he gave to the founding of the Livingstonia Mission, were an invaluable contribution to the fulfilment of Livingstone's dearest hope. James Stewart, therefore, must be named as the first, and one of the worthiest, of all who have followed in the footsteps of the great explorer.

I: *A Son of the Disruption*

He was born on February 14, 1831, in the city of Edinburgh, where his father was a cab proprietor. In 1842 the family removed to the farm of Pictonshill, near Scone in Perthshire, and this was their home till 1847 when they returned to Edinburgh. These five years cover the period of the Disruption, when religious feeling and controversy in Scotland were at fever heat. The farmer of Bictonshill was the mainstay of the Free Church in Scone. Meetings were held in his barn, where the country people sat breathless under the fervent preaching of Andrew Bonar and the saintly John Milne of Perth. When the Free Church of Scone was built, "Pictonshill" carted the stones free of charge, and in this labour of love his son James, then a schoolboy at Perth Academy, lent a willing hand in his holidays. It is pleasing to relate that the same autumn the villagers of Scone, to show their gratitude, insisted on reaping the fields of Pictonshill without hire.

In this time of religious quickening the ardent spirit of James Stewart took fire. One day as he followed the plough, his mind busy with the dreams of youth, the patient horses halted in the furrow, and there, leaning on the stilts, he brooded on his future till, suddenly straightening himself up, he said, "God helping me, I will be a missionary." Writing long after of his boyhood, he said, "Though from my earliest years I meant to go abroad, I cannot say that missionary work attracted me at first. The boy's ideal, firmly fixed and constantly recurring, was to lead an expedition in some unexplored region. That was probably nothing more than the mere restlessness of race-instinct in a boy half Norse on his mother's side, if also half Celt on the other." Nature and grace now combined to make him a knight errant of the Kingdom of God.

In 1847 his father, owing to money losses, gave up his farm and returned to business in Edinburgh. In this financial strait young Stewart gave his help for several years, and he was twenty before the way opened for him to go to the university. His curriculum, however, was extraordinarily complete and varied.

It embraced three full courses of four years each in Arts, Divinity and Medicine. His Arts and Divinity courses were taken at Edinburgh (1850-59), except two sessions at St. Andrews (1852-54). His medical studies were begun at Edinburgh (1859-61), and, after being interrupted by his adventurous trip to the Zambesi, were completed at Glasgow (1864-66). During the whole time he supported himself, at first by private tutoring, afterwards by preaching and secretarial work. His character and bearing seem to have left a vivid impression on the minds of his fellow students. Tall and thin,—his height was six feet two inches—full of wiry strength, with a long, eager stride that carried him forward as if he swooped on things, gifted with a fine mobile face and expressive eyes, and bearing himself with soldierly dignity, he made a distinguished figure in any company.

His home circle was early broken by death. He lost his mother when quite young and his father married again. After his father's death he lived for several years with his step-mother, who loved him like an only son. Their mutual affection was very rare and beautiful. She died, however, when he was a divinity student and he was left alone in the world. "What an affection she lavished upon me," he writes, "now I can never repay her. . . . Despite all my infirmity of temper, sometimes, alas too often, overcoming me, I loved my mother and she knew it."

II : *With Livingstone on the Zambesi*

Stewart's thoughts were definitely turned to Africa by Livingstone's visit to England in 1857 and the publication of his travels. He was then a divinity student. At the close of his course he intimated to the Foreign Mission Committee of the Free Church that he and two fellow students were willing to go as pioneer missionaries to the regions of Central Africa which Livingstone had opened up. This offer the committee, though interested in the proposal, felt compelled to decline. Most students would have considered such a refusal decisive, but Stewart was not built that way. He was tenacious and resolute, even to a fault, and difficulties, for him, existed only to be overcome. He had commenced his medical studies with a view to fitting himself more fully for service in Africa. Now he set to work and formed an influential committee, called the New Central Africa Committee. He raised subscriptions, threw his whole private means into the fund, and was commissioned by the committee to proceed to the Zambesi on a mission of inquiry.

He set sail in July, 1861, in the company of Mrs. Livingstone. Dr. Livingstone was at that time British consul on the Zambesi, and had just aided in planting the Universities' Mission in the Shire Highlands to the south of Lake Nyasa. Reinforcements were going out to strengthen that mission, including Bishop Mackenzie's sister and Mrs. Burrup, and a brig had been hired to convey the party from Durban to the Zambesi mouth. Both at Cape Town and at Durban Stewart was amazed to find himself the object of bitter attacks on the part of some who seemed determined that he should never reach the Zambesi. In certain quarters he was represented as a trader in the guise of a missionary. The Church of England authorities regarded him as a poacher on their preserves. Having commenced mission work the previous year at a single station, which they were to abandon the following year, they appeared to consider the whole of Central Africa as their diocese, and were ready to cry, "Hands off," to all other Christians. It was a pitiful exhibition of that exclusive spirit which the Church of England alone of Protestant Churches cherishes, and which is peculiarly detestable in the mission field. At Durban Stewart despaired of being permitted to go farther, but Mrs. Livingstone came to the rescue by declaring firmly that she would not go without him. So perforce he had to be allowed on board, and arrived off the mouth of the Zambesi where he was warmly welcomed by Livingstone on February 1, 1862.

For four months he was Livingstone's guest at Shupanga and received from him every encouragement in his project of planting a Scottish mission in Central Africa. In April Mrs. Livingstone died. Stewart was present on that sad occasion and at Livingstone's request commended her soul to God. Next day he helped to lay her body in the grave. In these circumstances the two men were drawn very closely together and spent the evenings in long, intimate talks. But the call of their work soon separated them. While Livingstone proceeded to the exploration of the Rovuma, Stewart got a canoe with eight rowers and pushed up the Shire. Then, leaving the canoe below the Murchison cataracts, he travelled on foot through the Shire Highlands, where Blantyre now stands. While recognising the natural fertility and healthiness of the country, he reports it "a lonely land of barbarism, of game and wild beasts, of timid and harried but not unkindly men, harassed by never ending slave raids and inter-tribal wars." It was a bitter disappointment that his resources did not permit him to reach Lake Nyasa, though he was within fifty miles of its southern end. Returning to the Zambesi he proceeded up that river past Tete as far as the Kebrabasa rapids. He did a great deal of hard tramping in examining the country on both sides of the river. Livingstone speaks of "the most praiseworthy energy with which he did all this in spite of occasional attacks of fever." Stewart himself wrote, "Considering the way we lived, the wonder is we were ever free from fever. We carried no tents but slept in the open when dry, and in the canoe when it rained. Except tea and coffee, we carried no civilised provisions, but depended mainly on what could be got in the country." So severely had the fever told upon him that, when he returned to the coast, Captain Wilson, from whom he had parted fifteen months before, failed completely to recognise him, and described him afterwards as being "more like a bag of bones than a man."

He returned to Scotland after an absence of nearly two and a half years, bringing with him a considerable amount of fresh and accurate information regarding the state of Central Africa and the prospects of Christian work there. He reported that the most hopeful line of advance appeared to be northward by the Shire to Lake Nyasa, not westward along the Zambesi. At the same time his view was that the disturbed state of the country made the planting of a mission for the moment impossible. The collapse of the Universities' Mission may have helped to this conclusion.

Livingstone thought it too hasty and continued to hope that Stewart would rejoin him on the Zambesi. It was not, however, until after Livingstone's death that Stewart's work bore fruit in the Livingstonia and Blantyre Missions.

III: *The Builder of Lovedale*

Meantime Stewart resumed and completed his medical studies at Glasgow. Thereafter he was appointed to Lovedale in South Africa. In November, 1866, he married Mina, youngest daughter of Alex. Stephen, shipbuilder, Glasgow, and together they reached Lovedale on January 2, 1867. In accepting this appointment Dr. Stewart had stipulated that whenever a new mission should be planted in Central Africa he should be free to join it. Seven long years were to elapse before that time came, seven years in which he struck his roots deep, and filled his hands with work that he could not forsake. So, although Dr. Stewart, as will presently appear, aided in founding and organising Livingstonia, it was at Lovedale that he found his life work, and reared an enduring monument to his name.

Lovedale lies about 80 miles inland from East London, in the northeast corner of Cape Colony, which is the ancient home of the Kafir race. In 1824 a mission was planted here by the Glasgow Missionary Society, and named Lovedale after Dr. Love, the first secretary of the Society. The site was a bare, open valley, through which the little river Tyumie flows, but it has been greatly beautified by planting and cultivation. As the Kafrarian mission developed a training school was established here in 1841, under the charge of the Rev. W. Govan. Thus when Dr. Stewart arrived Mr. Govan had been at work for over a quarter of a century with considerable success. The Institution had produced at least one student of distinction in Tiyo Soga, the preacher and writer, one of Africa's most eminent sons. In the late fifties, with the aid of Government grants, provision was made for industrial training as well as general education, and natives were apprenticed as carpenters and wagon-builders, masons and blacksmiths. Printing was added in 1861.

Lovedale was visited in 1864 by Dr. Duff, the famous Indian educationalist, who reported in favour of a considerable extension and reorganisation of the work. The Institution was based on the principle of equality, no distinction being made between the boys from the various tribes and different missions. A small minority of white pupils sat on the same benches as the Africans. Mr. Govan's idea was to provide at Lovedale, for such as were able to receive it, both natives and whites, an English High School education, including Latin and Greek. Dr. Duff had the fear that this policy tended to draw the school aside from its proper work of training native pastors and teachers. The matter was the subject of some controversy at the time, which eventually led to the resignation of Mr. Govan, shortly after Dr. Stewart arrived at Lovedale. The young missionary had therefore a free field in which to work for the development of the Institution.

No fitter man could have been found for the task. He was not without experience of Africa, and he had brooded on her needs and problems for years. He was a man who knew his own mind, bold in conception, swift and decisive in action, a tireless worker and a born administrator. The impression he made upon the natives was expressed in the name by which he became known among their tribes, *Somgxada,* the Swift Strider. If he had a fault it lay in the direction of being impetuous and, as some would have said, overbearing. But, if quick, he was also very tender. No matter what work he had on hand, the moment he heard of distress or sickness or death he was there to comfort and to help.

Here is a picture of him, printed indelibly on the heart of a little child. "My father was District Surgeon for some years at Alice, about a mile and a half from Lovedale. To me then, although a child, Dr. Stewart seemed a second St. John 'whom Jesus loved.' One evening about forty years ago, there was a hurried knocking at our hall door, and upon opening we found a recent acquaintance, whose husband, Major G——, was absent for a short time, standing with her little boy in her arms.

" 'Oh!' she cried, 'R—— has been bitten by a snake.'

"He was a dear little fellow about four years of age. He had been bitten in several places, as Mrs. G—— in her fright had fallen with him, and forehead, leg and hands all bore marks of the snake's malice. My father was away. What was to be done? We sent for Dr. Stewart. He came and stayed all night. I can see them now—Mrs. G—— on her knees by the bedside, and dear Dr. Stewart. He sucked every one of those wounds. . . . For the passing stranger whose mother-heart was crying so sorely, 'Let this cup pass,' for the wee unknown laddie, whose little life as compared to his was as naught, he took in the poison and saved the child."

The companion picture is as beautiful, and gives the happy sequel. Thirty years have passed away and Dr. Stewart is known and honoured in all the Churches. One day he is found in his study, playing with his little grandchild, so pleased and laughing because the little fellow is "making his fingers like Granddaddy, and Granddaddy is a bad boy too," and he won't have him taken away because "they are both enjoying themselves," he says. And the golden link that binds the stories is that the father of the little grandchild was the boy whose poisoned wounds Dr. Stewart had sucked.

The coming of Dr. Stewart brought new life to Lovedale, and under him the development of the Institution was so great as completely to dwarf all that had gone before. He discarded as useless the attempt to teach Latin and Greek. Some of the natives, ambitious for a display of learning, grumbled at this, but he maintained that English was their classic, and a sufficient mental discipline. A much more startling innovation was the introduction of fees. No one had yet dared to imagine that natives would be induced to pay for education. After a two days' palaver on the question Dr. Stewart carried his point. A man, Nyoka, whose name the doctor ever after remembered with gratitude, rose and said, "I will give £4 for my son." Others followed. Contrary to all expectation, so successful was the new policy that in the four years from

1870 to 1874 the number of pupils rose from 92 to 480, and the fees from nothing to £1300.

Dr. Stewart laid the greatest stress upon the dignity of manual labour. He strove to rouse the native from his ancestral indolence, and at the same time to guard against the conceit that education sometimes brings. His aim was to make him in every way a more capable and energetic man. Accordingly every afternoon at three o'clock the boys were paraded in work parties, and Dr. Stewart would often go out at their head armed with his spade. On one occasion a party of visitors who had come to see Lovedale when its fame had spread through all the Colony, found a gang of Kafir boys busily digging. They addressed the foreman of the gang who stood, spade in hand. "Is Dr. Stewart at home?" "Yes," was the reply. "Can you tell us where to find him?" "He is here. I am Dr. Stewart." Lovedale is perhaps the only College in the world where a gold medal is given for the best spadework.

Among these manifold activities the religious and missionary aim was ever kept supreme. Dr. Stewart felt a personal responsibility for seeing that no boy should drift through Lovedale without having the claims of Christ definitely brought before him. The senior students were encouraged to go out on Sunday morning and preach in the neighbouring kraals, and on Saturday evening Dr. Stewart was accustomed to meet with them and study the subjects of their addresses. Twice a year a week of special services was held at the Institution, in order to bring to decision those who had been under Christian teaching in the classes. Some of these occasions were memorable, notably in 1874 when Lovedale was visited by a wave of revival, doubtless due in some measure to sympathetic contact with the revival then in progress at home. One result of this movement was that when volunteers were asked for Livingstonia fourteen students offered themselves. On hearing this a doubter exclaimed, "Now I believe in the Lovedale revival. Before, I didn't."

IV: *The Spirit of the Fingoes*

Towards the close of his first period of service in Lovedale Dr. Stewart was suddenly faced with a great additional task. To the north of Lovedale, in the land beyond the Great Kei River, is the home of the Fingoes. They were the broken remnant of certain Zulu tribes who, for their loyalty to Britain, had been granted a settlement there. They had previously been degraded and enslaved by other tribes, but now, under the wise guidance of a British resident, Captain Blyth, they had begun to realise their manhood. Looking wistfully at Lovedale they at length in 1873 appealed to Dr. Stewart to plant among them a similar Institution, "a child of Lovedale," as they called it. Dr. Stewart had planned costly extensions at Lovedale and was on the eve of going home to raise the necessary money, so that this fresh appeal was embarrassing and might well have seemed impossible. Dr. Stewart started for Fingoland, but after a day's journey he turned aside into the house of a friend and wrote a letter to Captain Blyth proposing that if the Fingoes would themselves raise £1000, he would find another £1000. No such proposal had ever before been made to a native tribe, and Dr. Stewart was more than half inclined to think it would quench the ardour of the Fingoes. Three months later he received a telegram from Captain Blyth, *"Come up, the money is ready."* He lost no time in complying with this request, and his meeting with the Fingoes was as picturesque as it was historic. Thirty years later he described it thus: "The meeting to hand over that subscription was held at Ngqamakwe on the veldt, there being no building large enough for the crowd of men and women and missionaries. On a small deal table which stood on the grass was a large heap of silver, over £1450, and the substance of the native speaking that day was given in a sentence by one of themselves. He pointed to the money and said, 'There are the stones, now build.' Kafirs are all good speakers, figurative, concrete, pointed. There was further speaking, and the people were assured that their contribution would be covered by one of equal amount, to be raised in Scotland or elsewhere, and all went home satisfied that the institution was safe, as the sum of £3000 had been practically guaranteed."

During the progress of the building certain additions were considered necessary, and again the Fingoes rose to the occasion. Another meeting was held, more speeches were made, and a second £1500 in silver was subscribed. When the Institution was opened in 1877 there still remained a debt of £1600. On Sir Bartle Frere mentioning this to one of the headmen, he replied, "The thing is settled. We are going to pay all the debt." And they did. A final meeting was held at which, with considerable flourish of trumpets and abundant speechifying after the native fashion, amid a scene of great enthusiasm, shillings and half crowns were forthcoming in sufficient quantity to pay the debt. The institution was called Blythswood, in honour of Captain Blyth, and it has proved itself not only "a child of Lovedale," but the mother of civilisation in Fingoland. In 1890 it was declared by a competent observer that "the Fingoes of Transkei are half a century ahead of their countrymen in wealth, intelligence, and material progress, agricultural skill, sobriety, and civilised habits of life."

V: *The Birth of Livingstonia*

Dr. Stewart returned to Scotland early in 1874, having on hand the double task of raising £10,000 for Lovedale and £1500, according to his pledge, for Blythswood. At the moment he had no more thought of a mission in Central Africa, as he said afterwards, "than of proposing a mission to the North Pole." But the body of David Livingstone was brought home, and made its mute appeal to the Christians of Britain and of the world. On the 18th of April, 1874, Dr. Stewart took part in the funeral in Westminster Abbey, and the following month, at the General Assembly of the Free Church, he proposed, as Scotland's memorial of Livingstone, the founding of a mission in Central Africa. The closing sentence of his speech deserves to be quoted, as nobly describing the ideal of the mission, and giving public utterance for the first time to the historic name of Livingstonia. "I would humbly suggest, as the truest memorial of Livingstone, the establishment by this Church, or several Churches together, of an institution at once industrial and educational, to teach the truths of the Gospel and the arts of civilised life to the natives of the country, and that it be placed in a carefully selected and commanding spot in Central Africa, where from its position and capabilities it might grow into a town, and afterwards into a city, and become a great centre of commerce, civilisation, and Christianity. And this I would call Livingstonia."

The proposal was adopted with enthusiasm, but upon Dr. Stewart's willing shoulders fell the burden of raising the necessary £10;000. He set to work and speedily raised £20,000. So swiftly did things move that, exactly twelve months after the Assembly speech, the pioneer party under Mr. E. D. Young and Dr. Laws left for the Zambesi, carrying with them the little steamer *Ilala* for use on Lake Nyasa. No wonder Dr. Stewart, writing to his wife, says, "Livingstonia is the heaviest piece of business I have undertaken in my life. The responsibility is very great from the amount of money, life, and credit that is at stake."

He was not able to lead the pioneer party himself as he had to fulfil his obligations to Lovedale and Blythswood, but the summer of 1887 saw him back at Lovedale and ready to start for Central Africa with reinforcements for Livingstonia. In his party were four students of Lovedale, one of whom, William Koyi, is well entitled to be called the Apostle of Ngoniland. They reached Quilimane in August, sailed up the Zambesi and Shire in canoes, and, having accomplished the portages of the Murchison Cataracts, met the *Ilala* in the upper river and steamed into the lake. Dr. Stewart remained for fifteen months at Lake Nyasa till the new mission was fairly on its feet. Then he returned to Lovedale in the beginning of 1878. Thus he had given altogether five of the best years of his life to Central Africa.

VI: *The Triumph of Lovedale*

From this time onward Dr. Stewart devoted his strength to Lovedale, and under his powerful leadership the Institution was raised to the proud position which it occupies to-day as the glory of South African missions, and the rock that splinters the shafts of the missionary critic. All who would know what can be made of the native must visit it, and the visitor will carry away the most pleasant and inspiring memories. From the railway station of Alice one has a charming view of a well-wooded valley, with many roofs of scattered buildings rising over the trees. Then follows a mile of a drive between hedgerows of quince, and along a stately avenue. The spreading oaks and lofty pines, the flower and shrub plots, the trim turf and well kept gravel paths are a refreshing sight in a land of dreary veldt. At the head of the avenue stands the main building of the Institution, which contains a central hall with classrooms, library, and bookstore. To the right are the boys' dormitory and the dining hall, the workshops and technical buildings, and, in the distance, the Victoria Hospital. To the left, along a shady avenue, are the buildings of the girls' school. Scattered through the grounds are the teachers' houses, and, in the bottom of the valley, the Tyumie murmurs along between deep banks.

At Lovedale are gathered in hundreds the brightest of the native youth of South Africa. They belong to every tribe from the Cape to the Zambesi. Fingoes, Gaikas, Basutos, Zulus, Barolongs, Bechuanas, Metabele, are all mingled in friendly rivalry of work and sport. The six o'clock morning bell rings out ·over the valley, and soon the whole community is astir. A busy hum resounds through the classrooms and workshops till three o'clock in the afternoon, when there is a general parade for outdoor work which lasts till five. On Saturday the centre of interest is the "Oval," where many a keen game is contested. Sunday brings its own activities. By 6:30 in the morning little mission bands are on their way to preach in the neighbouring kraals. In the evening, when the sacred labours of the day are over, all assemble for worship in the central hall. To organise, superintend, and finance this great Institution was a Herculean task. The *Christian Express* of Lovedale thus described Dr. Stewart's activities: "He deemed fourteen, sixteen, or even eighteen hours of incessant toil a common daily task. He taught in the Institution, he edited this paper, he had medical charge of the Mission. In addition to week-day service he preached two sermons every Sabbath, he saw to every detail of the work, he guided every distinct department, he examined the classes, he superintended the field companies, he was here, there, and everywhere, tireless, commanding, inspiring. At a period when medical aid was difficult to obtain in the district, many were the calls made on his time and strength. Yet he gave both ungrudgingly, and no home was too far, no road too difficult, no night too stormy, to hinder the great missionary in his errands of mercy."

It seemed to some that he burdened himself unduly with details, and in his eagerness held the reins too much in his own hands. That is a common fault of great rulers, but Dr. Stewart was far from conforming to the type of the soulless autocrat. All Lovedale knew that he had a very tender heart. "My dear fellow," he exclaimed as he stood by the death-bed of one of his colleagues, "forgive me if ever I have seemed harsh, or have hurt you in any way." "I know nothing," was the reply, "but your great goodness to me and mine these many years."

He watched over his pupils with fatherly care. He had learned from Livingstone to respect the manhood of the natives, and he resented the contemptuous treatment they too often received from the colonists. "I am a father," he used to say, "and I wish to treat these children entrusted to me as I should like my own children to be treated if they were under the care of strangers."

His own home life was exceedingly happy, and none was readier than he to make merry with his children and his friends. It was said of him that "he could laugh tears." Some of his letters to his children remind one, in their tenderness, of Luther's letters to his little Hans. Thus he writes to his little girl, "I will tell you now what I am doing. I go about the streets and into the offices, and I say to this man, 'Give me a hundred pounds for Lovedale,' and to another who is not so rich I say, 'Give me fifty pounds.' And they give it because they love Christ and have already given Him their hearts. Now I am going to ask *you* to give Jesus something too. Go into the garden and see if there are any flowers. Then go into another garden and you will find a flower. Take it and say, 'Lord Jesus, I give you this. It is a little flower, it is **my** heart. I give it to you because you love me. You love me so much that long ago you died for me. And now I give the little flower of my life, and I pray to you,

> In the Kingdom of Thy grace
> Give a little child a place.'

And he will give you that place, and you will be a glad and happy little girl, and we shall be so happy when we hear that you have given this little flower to Christ."

The hospitality of the Stewarts was unbounded. A constant succession of visitors to Lovedale,—missionaries, educationalists, statesmen,—found an unfailing welcome. No less courteous a welcome was given to the native who came to the kitchen door, bringing some grievance or pitiful story. The old people of the Lovedale location were his special charge. Every Sunday there was a dinner-party of old men at the house, and if any were too feeble to come for it, the meal was sent to them. His friends used to say that "great as he was in action, he was greater still in sympathy."

One of his staff tells the following story: "An old

native man was living under the trees at Lovedale. He was a leper, cast out by his family, and almost starving. Dr. Stewart had a little hut built for him, and sent him food daily from his own house. The hut was was carried away by a flood. Dr. Stewart took a truck, put the old man on it, and with the aid of a boy carried him to an outhouse near his own, where he lived for several years. He was a heathen, but either Dr. Stewart or a native student read and prayed with him almost daily. Light dawned on his soul. I used to hear him pray every night."

Lovedale was so conspicuous a success that it naturally became a target for the critic of missions. Solemn warnings were given against the employment of Lovedale boys, who were declared to be raw Kafirs spoiled by education. The industrial side of the work especially was the object of bitter attack by those who wished to reserve all skilled labour to the white man. Dr. Stewart was therefore compelled to become the defender of his own system and the champion of native education. His defence was characteristically thorough and effective. In 1887 he published *Lovedale Past and Present,* in which he gave the record of over 2000 natives who had passed through the Institution. Of these 36 had become preachers, 409 teachers, 6 lawyers, 3 journalists, 26 telegraphists, while the rest were employed in various trades or in farming. Only three per cent had been brought before the magistrate for breaking the law. "Can Oxford do better than that?" Dr. Stewart was wont to say. In the year 1900 the record was brought up to date and again published. It then contained 6640 names, of whom preachers and teachers numbered 880, farmers 385, tradesmen 352, Government clerks 112, in railway and police work 86, while about 1000 were employed at the mines. It was a triumphant vindication of Lovedale. Dr. Stewart could truly say, "But for the education received here and the previous labours of the missionaries who sent them to Lovedale, they would have been unable to distinguish the top of a printed page from the bottom, unable to use a single tool, unable even to use that complicated instrument called a spade, as anyone may satisfy himself if he sends a raw native to dig in his garden. They have been dragged out of the abyss of ignorance and entire want of manual skill by the opportunities they have had in this and similar places."

Happily Dr. Stewart lived to see in 1905 the publication of an authoritative pronouncement in favour of native education by the African Native Affairs Commission. After an exhaustive inquiry they unanimously declared, "that the natives must be educated and civilised, that the only people who have tried to elevate them are the missionaries and some Christian families, and that the hope of their elevation must depend mainly on their acceptance of the Christian faith and morals."

VII: *The Founding of Kikuyu*

In 1891 Dr. Stewart was called to another big pioneering adventure, this time in British East Africa. Sir William Mackinnon and other friends, having subscribed money for an East African mission, asked Dr. Stewart to organise and establish it. He was at home on furlough, and now sixty-one years of age, but he responded to the call with the ardour of youth. Proceeding to Mombasa he organised a caravan and led it 200 miles up country, toiling through the Taro Desert till they reached the higher ground north of Kilima Njaro, where the mission was successfully established. It is now familiarly known as the Kikuyu mission of the Church of Scotland. Dr. Stewart's exertions on this occasion appear extraordinary for a man of his age. "It is safe to say," a colleague at the Institution wrote, "that during the thirteen days he spent at Lovedale when about to pioneer the East African Mission, he did not sleep thirty hours. When the dawn was breaking you could still see a light in his room." On the march he had to urge the parched and weary carriers forward, yet he was the only one in the party 'untouched by sickness and unmarked by fatigue.'"

VIII: *"Without Were Fightings"*

The last decade of Dr. Stewart's life was crowded with labours and troubles to an unusual degree. Towards the close of the century the Ethiopian movement wrought wide-spread havoc in the mission churches of South Africa. It had for its aim the establishing of a native church wholly independent of white control, but the movement was vitiated by race feeling and empty vanity. It did not touch Lovedale till 1898, when Mzimba, the pastor of the native church, an old pupil and friend of Dr. Stewart, seceded without warning, taking with him two-thirds of his congregation and £1300 of church money. How little cause Mzimba had to complain of his old teacher may be gathered from the fact that once when travelling together, on coming to an inn, Dr. Stewart insisted that, unless accommodation were found for Mzimba, he himself would sleep in the barn and let his native friend occupy his bedroom. The treachery of Mzimba, for it was no less, cut Dr. Stewart to the heart. All attempts at conciliation having failed, the Presbytery had to appeal to the law courts, and Mzimba was ordered to restore the money he had appropriated. The lawyer who conducted the case wrote afterwards, "Dr. Stewart was never the same man again. That bitter time left a scar upon his heart that I believe he felt each day until he died."

Another event which brought a dark cloud was the outbreak of the Boer War. Dr. Stewart had all his life kept himself free from party politics, but on this occasion he felt compelled to enter the arena. He believed, as did all missionaries in South Africa, that Kruger's Government was the enemy of native rights. He had sufficient evidence of his own to confirm the weighty verdict of Moffat and Livingstone and Mackenzie. He felt, therefore, that he ought not to be silent, especially as some Boer ministers had addressed a partisan appeal to the Churches of Britain. Accordingly he threw himself into the conflict in his own swift and impulsive way. It was the welfare of the natives that he had chiefly in view, but that seemed to many a negligible element in the historic struggle between Boer and Briton. It was a time of great political bitterness, and Dr. Stewart was deeply grieved to find that his action not only lost him the friendship of many of the Dutch for whom he cherished a warm regard, but also alienated some of his friends at home.

In 1899, the year preceding the Church Union **in** Scotland, Dr. Stewart was called to be Moderator of the Free Church, the first African missionary who had occupied that honourable position. In 1902 he was back in Scotland delivering the Duff lectures on missions, which were published the following year under the title of *Dawn in the Dark Continent*. After a visit to America he returned to Lovedale in 1904 and told the students, who met him with royal welcome, that he had come home to stay. Signs had appeared of heart weakness through overstrain, and he knew that the end of the journey could not be far off.

Nineteen hundred and five was the last year of his life, and it brought a fresh trouble of an alarming kind. The decision of the Scottish Church case having gone in favour of the Wee Frees, Mzimba, with the most complete effrontery, represented himself as an opponent of the Union, and put in a claim for Lovedale! Nobody knew better than the Wee Frees that Mzimba's case had nothing to do with the Union, they had themselves voted against him in the Free Church General Assembly, but now they warmly took his side and supported his claim. It would be difficult to find a more disgraceful compact. Extensions were in progress at Lovedale, but everything was brought to a stand, and Dr. Stewart was faced with the prospect of seeing the noble fruit of his lifework snatched from his hand and given to those who could not possibly make use of it. Fortunately the Court dismissed Mzimba's claim with the contempt it deserved. But the burden and anxiety of these last months hastened the end.

IX: *"God is Not Dead"*

He died on December 21, 1905, in his 75th year,—"our grand old man of Lovedale and of the Empire," as the *Cape Times* described him. He was buried on Christmas Day on the summit of Sandili's Kop, a prominent hill overlooking the Institution. The feelings of the natives were touchingly expressed in an address to Mrs. Stewart, "The friend of the natives is gone. To-day we are orphans. To-day we have no present help. The wings which were stretched over us are folded, the hands which were stretched out in aid of the native are resting. The eye which watched all danger is sleeping to-day, the voice which was raised in our behalf is still, and we are left sorrowful, amazed, troubled. But in our sorrow we say, 'God is not dead.' "

His thoughts were given to Africa to the last. "I wish," he said to his native secretary as he bade him farewell, "I wish I could have done more for your people and for Africa." But he had done much. Within a week of his death a Native Convention met at Lovedale to consider the question of establishing a Native College for South Africa. Dr. Stewart's last days were spent in making preparations for the Convention, which he regarded as in some measure the crowning of his lifework. The Convention opened with a memorial service at his grave, and thereafter it was resolved to urge the Colonial Governments to establish a central native university at Lovedale, to the support of which the natives pledged themselves to raise £50,000. Well might it be said of Dr. Stewart that he was *"felix opportunitate mortis,* favoured in the moment and manner of his death."

CHAPTER VI

LAWS OF LIVINGSTONIA

I: *Henry Drummond's Hero*

One midsummer evening in 1892 Prof. Henry Drummond presided over a meeting of Edinburgh students in the Oddfellows' Hall. In introducing the speaker he declared that "no man in Europe was better worth listening to." He was the first man to place a steamer on a Central African lake, "and I have often wondered what his feelings were as his vessel ploughed the virgin waters of the Lake." With moving eloquence Drummond spoke of the glory of the work, carried on for nearly twenty years "in a beastly climate." The speaker rose, a rugged, burly form, in striking contast to the elegant figure and delicate complexion of the Professor. Plainly he did not recognise the pen-portrait of himself that had been drawn. One had no time to think of the glory of the work, he said, it was just a case of pegging away in one's shirt sleeves from day to day. As for the climate, well—(with a dry smile breaking over his face, and pointing at Drummond with his thumb) "Look at him and look at me, and judge for yourselves."

Then he began to talk, not with eloquence or fluency, but the plain, downright talk of a strong man. On and on it flowed, till the daylight faded and faces were lost in the gloom. Then he abruptly stopped and apologised almost abjectly for having kept the meeting so long. It was Laws of Livingstonia, who since then has added another thirty years to his record of service, and has seen and done more wonderful things than, perhaps, any other living man.

II: *Dedicated from Birth*

Robert Laws was born in Aberdeen on May 28, 1851. He was an only child, and, his mother having died when he was but two years old, he was brought up by a somewhat stern step-mother, who nevertheless cherished a warm affection for the boy. His father was a cabinet-maker, a devout man whose early ambition of being a missionary had been frustrated, and who now dedicated his son from birth to the foreign field. Between father and son there was, in this as in other things, the most perfect sympathy. The boy's imagination was fired by reading Livingstone's *Travels,* and the secret prayer of his heart was, "O God, send me to the Makololo." Years afterwards he remembered that prayer when he met some of Livingstone's Makololo in the Shire Highlands and received their help in carrying the *Ilala* past the Murchison Cataracts.

Owing to the straitened circumstances of the family his way did not immediately open up, and he was apprenticed as a cabinetmaker. Even after he went to college he continued to work at his trade. His old shopmates he never forgot, and he used to visit some of them whenever he returned to Aberdeen. And they appreciated the man and his work. One of them as he lay dying said to his wife, "Send all my tools out to Dr. Laws."

The story of his early struggles bears a remarkable resemblance to that of David Livingstone, his hero and predecessor, in the same long hours of manual labour, followed by evening classes and night study. By the aid of a small bursary he was at length able to enter the University. The curriculum he planned was characteristically arduous and thorough. It was, by dove-tailing the classes, to take a complete course in Arts, Medicine, and Divinity in seven years. By sheer hard work and tireless plodding he carried it through.

During the winter of 1871, when worn down by his studies, he contracted smallpox and lay for weeks in a hospital at death's door. This illness had a curious sequel, for two years after, on applying for work under the Glasgow City Mission, he was appointed missionary to the Smallpox Hospital, a post which no one else could be found to undertake. Here he passed through a strenuous period of service, for an epidemic was raging in the city and the hospital was over-crowded. The Directors speak of his "praise-worthy devotion," but he had to live a sort of hermit life, shunned by most as a leper. One day at the end of May, 1874, he read in the *Glasgow Herald* a report of Dr. Stewart's proposal to the Free Church Assembly to found a mission in Central Africa as a memorial to David Livingstone. Instantly the conviction flashed through his mind, "This is the work I have been preparing for all my life." Some months later he met Dr. Stewart who, on his part, said, "This is my man if I can get him." Laws felt himself honour-bound to his own, the United Presbyterian, Church. The difficulty, however, was speedily overcome by that Church lending him to the new mission, while one of its Edinburgh congregations agreed to pay his salary for five years at least. It was a noble loan, never recalled, and a happy augury of the time when the two Churches would be joined in one.

The winter of 1874 was a busy time, for Laws had to pass his finals in Medicine and Divinity, besides helping in the preparations for the new mission. In April, 1875, he took his degree in Medicine and was ordained to the ministry, and on May 21st he sailed for Africa.

III: *Up the Zambesi to Lake Nyasa*

The original mission party went out under the guidance of Mr. E. D. Young of the Royal Navy, who had aided Livingstone in his exploration of the Zambesi. Besides Laws and Young, the party consisted of an engineer, a seaman, an agriculturist, a carpenter, and a blacksmith. Accompanying them was Mr. Henderson of the Church of Scotland who was sent out to prospect for a suitable site for a sister mission. Dr. Laws has long survived all his fellow pioneers. On the roll of honour of the Livingstonia mission his name stands first and is followed by no fewer than thirty-three names of fellow-workers, all of whom have passed from the service of the Mission. Thirty-fifth on the list appears the illustrious name of Dr. Elmslie, the oldest of his present colleagues.

On July 23, 1875, the mission party landed at the Kongone mouth of the Zambesi. Their little steamer, the *Ilala,* which they had brought out in parts, was speedily bolted together and launched. The up-river voyage proved an affair of great toil and difficulty. Sandbanks and *sudd* made progress slow, while crocodiles and hippos added more than a spice of danger. The junction of the Shire and the Zambesi was hidden in a maze of sluggish backwaters, but at length it was discovered and the *Ilala* steamed northward for the Lake. Now, however, a new obstacle intervened in the shape of sixty miles of cataract, where the river plunges down through the glens of the Shire Highlands. Fortunately in this district some of Livingstone's Makololo had established themselves in authority, and with their friendly help a thousand carriers were assembled, the boat was carried piecemeal over the hills, rebuilt and launched on the upper Shire. On October 12 at daybreak the *Ilala* sailed into the Lake, the first steamer to appear on any of the great inland seas of Africa. The glorious morning sun, just risen above the rim of the eastern hills, and flooding the surface of the Lake with its golden rays, seemed an emblem of the dawn of the Sun of Righteousness over these dark regions. As the prow of the little steamer cut into the virgin waters the engine was stopped and the company of pioneers, standing together on the after deck, sang the Hundredth Psalm. The same evening a landing was made on the white sandy beach at Cape Maclear, a promontory at the south end of the Lake.

IV: *The Beacon at Cape Maclear*

Lake Nyasa, as Dr. Laws discovered, is 360 miles long and 40 miles broad on an average. It is, in fact, a gigantic trench running north and south among the hills, and its surface is 1500 feet above sea level. The water is deep blue, the surrounding hills rise steeply from the shore, and near the south end especially there are exquisitely beautiful bays and inlets. The country lying to the west of the Lake may be divided into four parallel strips which also run north and south. First there is the Lake shore; second, the mountainous region of Ngoniland; third, the broad valley of the Luangwa, a tributary of the Zambesi, and fourth, the great plateau which forms the watershed of Central Africa, beyond which, to the west, lie Lake Bangweolo and the head waters of the Congo. The two mountain ranges bend round and unite at the north end of the Luangwa valley, thus forming a great horseshoe of hill country. This was the region now destined to become famous in missionary history as Livingstonia.

Darkest Africa was in those days no poetic name, but a most gruesome reality. Besides the usual horrors of African heathenism, the witch doctor, the poison ordeal, and the burial of the living with the dead, Nyasaland suffered from the two scourges of tribal war and slave raiding. The Angoni, a fierce tribe of Zulu origin, after many wanderings had settled on the plateau above the Lake, and were continually at war with the neighbouring tribes. Arab slave raiders from Zanzibar systematically scoured the country, and either by purchase or by violence secured multitudes of slaves, whom they sent down to the coast. There were regular slave ferries on the Lake, at Deep Bay, Kota Kota and other convenient points, where it was estimated that 40,000 slaves were shipped across. This nefarious traffic, more even than the Angoni raids, impoverished and devastated the land. These were the evils which had wrung from Livingstone's lips, a few years before, the bitter cry, "Blood, blood, everywhere blood."

Into the midst of this hell upon earth Dr. Laws and his colleagues came, and began the seemingly hopeless task of changing it into a garden of God. Temporary buildings were erected and a beginning made in acquiring the language and teaching the natives by simple pictures. It was painfully slow work. The natives at first could not even see a picture. "This is a cow," said the Doctor, pointing to the page. The announcement was received with shouts of derisive laughter. "But it *is* a cow. See its head, its legs, its tail." At last a precocious youth had the eyes of his understanding opened, and suddenly leaping body high, he exclaimed, "It is a cow. I see it." Such was the dawn of education in Nyasaland.

The Mission party had received orders, out of regard for the spiritual nature of their work, not to embroil themselves with the marauding tribes or the slave raiders, but while this policy was strictly adhered to, the Union Jack at the masthead of the *Ilala* had for a time a restraining influence on the Arabs, and the settlement at Cape Maclear became a city of refuge for the oppressed. By and by enemies grew bolder, threats and alarms of war were constant, and natives who were working at the Mission station were kidnapped.

For over a year the party at the Lake were without news of the outside world. Henderson had gone south to look for a suitable station in the Shire Highlands, and lay the foundations of the Blantyre Mission of the Church of Scotland. At length, in October, 1876, news arrived of the approach of reinforcements both for Blantyre and Livingstonia. At the head of the Livingstonia party was Dr. Stewart, accompanied by Dr. Black, a young medical missionary who was destined in a few weeks to fill the first grave at Cape Maclear. With them came three artisan missionaries and four native teachers from Lovedale, the most notable of whom was William Koyi. For the next eighteen months Dr. Stewart took charge of the mission and by his energy and experience aided greatly in its establishment.

As if their hands were not full enough at Cape Maclear, an urgent appeal for help came from Henderson in December. Blantyre seemed on the verge of collapse. The Livingstonia men responded to the appeal and, taking service in turns, became the real founders of the Church of Scotland Mission. It was while voyaging on the lower river, bringing up Blantyre goods from the coast, that Dr. Laws had his first serious illness and was brought to the point of death. Lying in his canoe, drenched with rain and sweat, sick and vomiting, suffering from dysentery and tortured by mosquitoes, he passed "the most miserable night of his life." Days of delirium followed, but he pulled through and struggled back to the Lake which already he felt to be like home.

Dr. Laws had circumnavigated the Lake soon after his first arrival, but Dr. Stewart and he now made a more thorough exploration of its coasts. They agreed that when the time was ripe for a forward movement from Cape Maclear it should be up the Lake to a point somewhere about the middle of its western side.

Dr. Stewart left for Lovedale in December, 1877, and henceforth Dr. Laws was in full charge of the Mission. The responsibility was no light one. Already three graves had been dug beneath the cliff at Cape Maclear. The Mission was an isolated outpost in the heart of heathenism, cut off from all civilised government and entirely thrown upon its own resources. Not the least difficult of the problems that faced the missionaries was how to maintain discipline among the natives at the station and protect themselves against malefactors. At Blantyre the missionaries took the administration of the law into their own hands with the most disastrous results. Dr. Laws, with more patience and prudence, appealed to the authority of neighbouring chiefs, or formed a court of headmen.

Anxious to extend his knowledge of the country, he went on a three months' journey up through the hills on the west side of the Lake, and made the acquaintance of the southern section of the Angoni. In this expedition he was greatly aided by William Koyi, who found that the Angoni still retained enough of their ancestral Zulu speech to understand him. This was a piece of great good fortune for William Koyi was welcomed as a fellow-tribesman, and, settling soon after in Ngoniland, he was honoured of God to break ground there for the Gospel. Next dry season Dr. Laws made a journey to North Ngoniland, going up the Lake to Bandawe and striking inland to the hills. Here he met Mombera, the paramount chief of the Angoni, and held friendly conference with that savage potentate. Mombera was not unfavourable to having a white man in his country, but he demanded that Dr. Laws should have no dealing with his enemies at the Lake shore. This of course could not be agreed to, and for long it continued to be a grievance with the Angoni.

In 1879 Dr. Laws journeyed down to the coast and sailed for East London with the pleasant expectation of meeting his bride. While waiting, he paid a visit to Lovedale to study the methods of native education there, and when he left the Colony he took with him about £30 in small change in the hope of inducing the natives of Nyasaland to use English money. Learning that his bride had come out by the east coast he hurried back to the Zambesi, only to find that she had already started up the river. He followed, with such speed as may be imagined, and overtook the lady at Blantyre where they were happily married. Mrs. Laws was the first white lady to live at Lake Nyasa, and for forty-two years, with incomparable courage and endurance, she braved storm and shine by her husband's side, till in the autumn of 1921 she was laid to rest beside Old Machar Cathedral in her native city of Aberdeen.

V: *Over the Graves of the Fallen*

Amid many difficulties and dangers the work at Cape Maclear went steadily on, but six long years passed ere the first convert was baptised. These years were a supreme trial to faith, for besides other discouragements there was much sickness, and four of the missionaries died. Cape Maclear had never been regarded as the permanent home of the Mission. It was not more unhealthy, perhaps, than any similar site on the Lake shore, but it was not central, and the presence of the tsetse fly in the immediate neighbourhood made agricultural development impossible. Accordingly a new site was chosen at Bandawe, half way up the west side of the Lake, and here the Mission settled in 1881.

This removal has been touchingly depicted as a tragedy and a defeat. Travellers who came expecting to find a hive of industry found Cape Maclear a place of graves and read in them disaster. No such feeling was in the heart of the great pioneer. To him Bandawe marked a big advance. Six months before the removal the first fruits of Darkest Africa had been reaped. The event is thus recorded in the Mission Journal: "*Sabbath, March 27th.*—This is a red-letter day in the history of the Livingstonia Mission. By the blessing of God the work of the past years has not been for naught, nor has He suffered His word to fail. For long we here have been seeing the working of God's word in the hearts of not a few, and now, by God's grace, one has been enabled to seek baptism as a public confession of his faith in Jesus Christ." The convert referred to was Albert Namalambe, who continued to carry on the work at Cape Maclear till it was taken over by the Dutch Reformed Church, which has now a mission in Nyasaland.

In the year of the removal to Bandawe another event of a different sort greatly widened the horizon of the Mission. This was the construction of the Stevenson Road. From the first Dr. Laws had been anxious to develop legitimate commerce as an antidote to the slave trade, and accordingly the African Lakes Corporation, formed three years previously to aid the Mission by opening up the country and developing its resources, had begun to make its presence beneficially felt in Nyasaland. One of its promoters, Mr. James Stevenson, offered £4000 for the construction of a road from the north end of Lake Nyasa to the south end of Lake Tanganyika, one condition being that a mission station should be planted on this highway into the far interior. The offer was gratefully accepted, and within a year of the removal to Bandawe, a new station was opened at Iwanda, on the line of the Stevenson Road. It was characteristic of the indomitable spirit of Dr. Laws thus to sound an advance over the graves of the fallen, and, as the conflict thickened round him, to have only the one desire, to "engage the enemy more closely."

VI: *Toil and Trial at Bandawe*

The years spent at Bandawe from 1881 to 1891 were a period of tremendous strain, under which many noble workers broke down. Some died in harness, others were invalided home, until at length Dr. Laws was left alone of all who had laboured at Cape Maclear. The ranks of the mission were kept steadily filled by fresh volunteers from home, chief of whom may be mentioned Dr. Elmslie who came out in 1885, and was honoured of God to become the Apostle of Ngoniland.

Bandawe had been chosen as the Mission centre because here the hills sweep back from the Lake, leaving a wide flat, which is thickly covered by the villages of the Atonga. These unhappy people, like all the dwellers on the Lake shore, were continually harassed by the wild Angoni raiders from the hills. So desperate was their condition that their villages were hidden in the most secret and inaccessible places, or built on piles driven into the Lake. Sir H. H. Johnston, the British Commissioner, reported to the Foreign Office in 1894 that, "but for the intervention of the Livingstonia missionaries, the Atonga would have been almost wiped out of existence by the raids of the Angoni." A similar testimony is given by the Atonga themselves. As an old chief feelingly expressed it, "We hoed our gardens in the strength of Dr. Laws."

It was only by an extraordinary display of courage and tact that this desperate situation was remedied. For years Dr. Laws at Bandawe and Dr. Elmslie up in the hills were more or less in daily peril. The work of evangelisation was heartbreakingly slow. In 1888 Dr. Laws reported that "up till now no native of Bandawe or the district has yet been baptised, though one from Cape Maclear was." This may be regarded as the darkest hour before the dawn, for about this time the Mission was plunged into an overwhelming sea of troubles.

The rainy season of 1886-87 had reaped a terrible harvest of death. At one time not a single worker in the field was free of fever. News came down from Iwanda that, of the three workers there, Dr. Kerr Cross was prostrate with fever, and Mrs. Cross and Mr. Mackintosh were dead. Dr. and Mrs. Elmslie were reported ill at Njuyu. At Bandawe Dr. and Mrs. Laws had fever and their baby was believed to be dying. The other workers on the station were in no better state. Then, as if the place were a public hospital, two hunters stricken down with fever were carried in. About the same time a boat came across the Lake from Likoma, where the Universities' Mission had now established themselves, bringing an invalid, Rev. G. H. Swinny, for medical care. Dr. Laws, with a temperature over 100° and hardly able to keep on his feet, tended the sick, and with his own hands made coffins for the dead.

"You are nearing home," he said gently to Mr. Swinny.

"Yes, Doctor, I know. It is the land I have long desired. Will it be convenient for you to bury me to-morrow?"

Convenient! What a world of Christian faith and hope and charity in that one word. Such is the spirit of the Church's pioneers, such the price at which the heathen world is won. "These lonely nights of watching on the Lake," said Dr. Laws, "have burned themselves forever into my heart."

In 1887 the Ngoni peril became so acute that most of the Mission property at Bandawe was shipped to Cape Maclear. Dr. Elmslie buried his medicines under the floor of his house at Njuyu, and the missionaries held themselves ready to escape at a moment's notice. Had it come to the worst escape would have been well-nigh hopeless. Even at Bandawe armed guards were posted between the mission houses and the beach to cut off retreat. One never-to-be-forgotten night, when sleep was not to be thought of, Dr. Laws, peering anxiously out, could see the dim figures of these savage sentinels, and then he heard in the next room his wife pacing the floor with her baby in her arms, and softly singing "The Lord's My Shepherd." It sounded like the voice of an angel, and filled his heart with the peace of God.

In that year also there came a big revival of the slave trade. It was occasioned by the appearance, at the north end of the Lake, of Mlozi, the most formidable of all the slave raiders, who entrenched himself near Karonga, cut the Stevenson Road below Iwanda, and harried the whole surrounding country. He waged war on the African Lakes Corporation, and, in spite of their heroic defence of Karonga, he seemed likely to succeed in his declared intention of clearing the white man out of the country. One horrible scene was enacted near a lagoon to the north of Karonga. The fugitive Wankonde having taken refuge in the tall reeds and grass by the Lake shore, Mlozi's men set fire to the reeds and burned them out. Those who fled the flames were shot or speared, while those who plunged into the water fell a prey to the crocodiles which had swarmed to the horrid feast. Captain (afterwards Sir Fred.) Lugard took part in the fighting with Mlozi, of which he has given a full account in his *Rise of Our*

East African Empire. Being shot through both arms he spent some weeks of convalescence at Bandawe. Many years afterwards he wrote, "I have seen many missions since those days on Lake Nyasa, but yours remains my ideal mission, because it is so free from ostentation, and carries out so effective and thorough a work on such sound, practical lines."

To crown these troubles, in the same dark year the Portuguese asserted a claim to the whole of Nyasaland, closed the Zambesi waterway, and sent an army of conquest up the Shire. The Mission was thus in the position of an army attacked in front and flank and suddenly finding its line of communications cut. It was a crisis to test the stoutest heart, but Dr. Laws never flinched nor had any thought but of holding out to the last.

The crisis passed, and in a marvellously short time a complete change became visible in Nyasaland. God's hand turned darkness into dawn. The solid phalanx of heathenism began to show signs of breaking up, the forces of the Gospel triumphed in Ngoniland, and in 1890 there came a season of rich blessing there. Vast multitudes assembled, not now to plan a bloody raid, but to hear the message of peace. They who before were the terror of the country, the Prussians of Nyasaland, became the sweet singers of Central Africa. The very war-song they were wont to sing when they sent round the fiery cross among the tribesmen was now set to Gospel words which summon fathers and sons to the banner of Christ.

Then Britain, roused at last by the urgent appeals of the Home Church, sent an ultimatum to Portugal, and in 1891 declared a protectorate over Nyasaland. This sealed the slave raiders' doom, and the inhuman traffic was finally ended in 1895, when Mlozi was tried and hanged for his many crimes. In the words of the old chief of the Wiwa, "All the people said, 'It is good.'"

Ere Dr. Laws left Bandawe in 1891 the foundations of a Christian Church were firmly laid there, and in the following year his successor began to reap an abundant harvest of his years of patient sowing. At a Livingstone Centenary meeting held at Bandawe, Vyamba, a venerable tribesman, told how Dr. Laws at first had said, "Yes, war is thick enough about you, but it will not last for ever. You pray to God about it and see what happens.'

" 'The white man lies,' said we.

" 'No,' said the Doctor, 'it is not lies.'

"And now," concluded the speaker with a thrill that went through his audience, "look here today. My heart warms. Jesus has been the life of us."

VII: *A Marvellous Transformation*

In 1891 Dr. Laws, whose health had been causing grave anxiety, left for Scotland in obedience to a peremptory summons from the Home Committee. On this furlough he laid before the Church his plans for an educational institution which might be •to Central Africa what Lovedale was to South Africa. He travelled extensively in America, inspecting technical and agricultural colleges as well as any institutions or works where new and helpful ideas were likely to be picked up. Returning to Scotland he was sent as a deputy to the Calabar Mission in Nigeria to report on the possibilities of a training institution there. While in Calabar he received a strong impression of the deadliness of the west coast climate and of the heroism of the men and women who under such conditions carried on the work. One of his fever patients was the famous Mary Slessor. "It was not to be wondered at," he wrote, "seeing that she started by night and walked to Creek Town, reached it at 5 a.m. dripping wet, got a change, some milk she needed, and was away in a canoe at 7 a.m." On the basis of Dr. Laws' report the Duke Town Institution was established in Calabar, and continues to flourish.

His so-called furlough over, Dr. Laws returned to Nyasaland in 1894, taking with him a band of young and valuable recruits for the Mission, including James Henderson, now Principal of Lovedale. It had been agreed by the Committee before he left that he should now look for a suitable site for the Institution which he had planned, and which was to bear, by preeminence, the name of Livingstonia. No time was lost in setting about the work. In September Dr. Laws and Dr. Elmslie went prospecting among the hills towards the north end of the Lake. They were old friends and comrades in arms, who had been through many trials and perils together. Next to their religious faith the thing that had sustained them was their sense of humour. The quiet chuckle of Dr. Laws was ever ready to bubble up in response to the great ringing laugh of Dr. Elmslie. Once it marked the turning point in a life and death struggle. Dr. Laws was down with fever at Bandawe and believed himself dying. Dr. Elmslie hurried down from the hills to his help, but in spite of all that skill and care could do, the patient's strength seemed gone. Dr. Elmslie commended his soul in prayer to God, then, moved by a sudden impulse, gave him a dig in the ribs. Dr. Laws responded with a laugh, and from that moment began to recover.

Travelling northwards they made a thorough exploration of the hills and valleys behind Mt. Waller. One night their camp was attacked by several lions, one of which sprang with a roar on Dr. Laws' tent and tore open the side. Dr. Elmslie, awaking suddenly and seeing the great rent, thought for one horrible moment that the lion had made off with its victim, but a shout from the interior of the tent reassured him. As he said afterwards, "It was the most welcome sound I ever heard."

Mt. Waller is a bold, altar-shaped promontory towering above Lake Nyasa towards its northern end. Near it, there is a little plateau with a precipitous descent to the Lake, and richly wooded hills rising up behind. Here seemed the most promising site for the Institution. Two streams, the Manchewe and the Kazichi, pouring over the cliff in cataracts side by side, gave assurance of an abundant water supply. Behind the waterfalls are some low caves, in which the miserable natives were found to be hiding through fear of the Angoni. Dr. Laws crept in on his hands and knees to make their acquaintance. Seeing him burrowing like a terrier in a rabbit's hole, Dr. Elmslie announced with mock gravity, "Dr. Laws looking for a site for the Institution." "Well," was the retort, "could I be in a better attitude than on my knees?"

It would be difficult, perhaps impossible, to find on the face of the earth a spot where so dramatic and beneficent a change has been wrought within living memory. On the summit of the plateau, immediately above these hidden caves and dwellings, the Livingstonia Institution now stands. It is an extraordinary achievement, planted there in the heart of the wilds. Savage nature surges up to the very doors. Around it are forests and jungle where lions and leopards, elephants and rhinos freely roam; some thousands of feet below glitters the blue Lake, whose shores are the haunt of the crocodile and hippopotamus. But on the plateau itself, how marvellous a transformation! A road has been built from the Lake shore which, twisting round corners, striding across ravines, clinging to the very face of the cliff, climbs up hand over hand to the top. An avenue, planted with Mlanje cedar, runs along the summit, leaving space for a line of buildings between it and the cliff edge. Here are the school, the hospital and the teachers' houses. Opposite are the post-office and the workshops, where engineering, carpentry, printing, etc., are taught. Elsewhere on the plateau are to be found a farmsteading and meal-mill, a saw-mill, a brickwork and a pottery. Through the liberality of Lord Overtoun, a lifelong friend of Livingstonia, a water supply has been brought from the hills and turbines have been erected at the falls to generate electric light and power for all the buildings. To the natives it was a crowning evidence of the white man's magic that he was able to make water run up-hill and light his house by pressing a button.

The buildings of the Institution are plain in the extreme, but the plan is spacious, leaving room for future development. Everywhere there is evidence of a master mind with far-sweeping vision and profound faith in the future. One finds in Dr. Laws a mind capable at once of grasping a great conception and of patiently working out the minutest details. Of the latter quality the following instance may perhaps be given. Entering a room where a native servant had laid the mat awry, he pounced down upon it and put it straight. Then looking up almost bashfully, he said in half-humourous self-defence, "People won't believe it, but you give the African a great lift when you teach him just to put things straight." Perhaps no fitter description could be given of his own life's work than simply that—"teaching the African to put things straight." His forty-odd years in Central Africa have been largely occupied with trivial duties, yet he has laboured with immense cumulative effect and put many things straight in Nyasaland.

Not content with his vast achievements he dreams of a more glorious future. Early one morning he led the writer into a thicket on the highest part of the plateau.

"Here," he said, "is the site of the Overtoun Memorial Church, where the clock on the tower will be seen for miles around."

Then, boring deeper into the thicket and standing up to the knees in the dewy grass, he waved his hands towards the surrounding trees, saying, "Here is the site of the permanent college buildings, and this is the quadrangle."

A few moments later he emerged from the thicket and, standing in the open, looked eastward over a wide panorama of wooded hills and valleys, all of it the property of the Institution, the princely gift of the British South Africa Company.

"The Home Committee," he said, "were very reluctant to be saddled with all this land, but the day is coming when it will be of great value. You know," he continued, speaking as one Aberdeen student to another, "what a blessing the Aberdeen University bursaries have been to the poor students of the north of Scotland. Where did the funds come from? Much of it from lands gifted long ago to the University, not of great value at the time, but now a rich endowment. So will it be with these lands."

As one listened one could foresee, in the light of the old man's faith and vision, the Institution becoming the University of Central Africa, and the keen-minded lads from all the surrounding tribes flocking up to its bursary competition.

VIII : *The Crowning Years*

The years from 1894 were years of steady expansion in the Mission. The opening of the stations at Karonga and Mwenzo carried the field of operations up to the frontier of German East Africa. Kasungu and Loudon became centres of activity in South Ngoniland, from which the country was evangelised westward into the valley of the Luangwa. More recently a far outpost beyond the Luangwa was established at Chitambo among the people where Livingstone died, while from Mwenzo an advance was made southward along the Rhodesian plateau to Chinsali, near the Lubwa River.

These developments, when studied geographically, reveal a strategy Pauline in its boldness. The advance was not made timidly from village to village, but central positions were occupied from which whole tribes could be evangelised. The average distance between the stations was seventy to a hundred miles, and round each of these centres there was gradually formed a wide network of out-stations, amounting in some cases to over a hundred. This steady expansion was accompanied by a bountiful spiritual harvest, with occasional tidal waves of revival, which commanded the attention of the whole Christian world, and made Livingstonia famous as one of the most wonderful triumphs of modern missions.

The dominant influence of the Mission in Nyasaland may be gathered from an important political event which occurred in 1904. British authority had been established for years in South Nyasaland, but the Angoni had been left severely alone, that nation of warriors being regarded as a hornet's nest, not to be lightly disturbed. Meantime the Gospel was making progress among them, and there was a growing desire to be incorporated in the British Empire. Sir Alfred Sharpe, the Governor of Nyasaland, relied implicitly on Dr. Laws' advice, and the event justified his confidence. On September 2 he made a peaceful entry into Ngoniland, accompanied only by Lady Sharpe and a few attendants, and after friendly conference with the chiefs received their willing allegiance. Writing to Dr. Laws of this remarkable event he said, "I was surprised to find the Chiefs already quite prepared, if not even glad, to accept the new condition of affairs. This is undoubtedly largely due to the influence exercised by your people." The Angoni, let it be remembered, are come of the same stock as the Zulus and the Matabele, whose contact with the British Empire is a record of costly and bloody wars. If the question be asked, "Why is the history of Ngoniland so different?" there is only one possible answer—Livingstonia.

In 1908 Dr. Laws was called home to be Moderator of the General Assembly of the United Free Church. He obeyed with some reluctance, for court functions and ecclesiastical ceremonial were not in his line. But when he took the chair it did the Church good to see him, this weather-beaten pioneer, this man of his hands, and to hear his words, so straightforward and unadorned. Speaking to the young missionaries on Consecration Night, he said, "After thirty-three years of a rough and tumble experience, which I hope it will never be your lot to know, I can only say that if I had my choice, and even knowing what was before me, I would go forth to-day to the missionary field." Although busy throughout the year addressing meetings up and down the country and discharging the duties of his office, he found time for studies at Edinburgh University in bacteriology and tropical diseases.

Returning to Central Africa in 1909, he resumed his labours with unflagging zeal, and the work of God prospered in his hand. In 1914, before the outbreak of the war, the report of Livingstonia stated that there were 14 organised congregations with 741 out-stations, having in connection with them a Christian community of over 38,000 souls. The number of schools was 907, and of scholars almost 60,000. Native evangelists, elders and deacons share in the oversight of the congregations, and the whole is organised into a Presbytery which forms, with Blantyre Mission, the *Church of Central Africa Presbyterian*. That these many thousands have not been hastily gathered in, without due care and examination, may be judged from the fact that every candidate must spend four years under Christian instruction, must learn to read, and finally must receive the approval of the native elders before admission to full membership.

In May, 1914, a historic assembly met in Bandawe, the mother station of the Mission. It was the occasion of the annual meeting of the Mission Council and Presbytery, but was made specially memorable by the ordination of the first three native pastors. The Council and Presbytery met daily for a week and discussed such grave questions as the law of Christian marriage, the creed and government of the Church, and the support of the ministry. Native elders took their full share in the discussions, and appeared to realise the responsibility resting on them to lay the foundations of the Christian social order of the future. At the ordination service the spacious church was crowded. Atonga and Angoni mingled in their thousands, and so vast was the concourse of people that admission to the church had to be regulated by ticket. Of the three pastors to be ordained, one was a Tonga, the other two Angoni. All three were men fully trained and thoroughly tested by years of faithful service. They knelt down side by side and Dr. Laws laid his hands on them, with the hands of the Presbytery, and ordained them, once mortal foes, now to be brother ministers of the Gospel of Christ. It was a scene which could never be forgotten by those who were privileged to behold it. At the close of the service the writer asked Dr. Laws if he had ever dreamed of such a day as this.

"Yes," he replied with animation, "I knew it would come. Never in the darkest day did I doubt it."

"But did you expect you would live to see it?"

He smiled, "Ah, that is another question."

Not often is a heroic life so gloriously crowned. Well might he have sung his *Nunc Dimittis*. Forty long years before, in the might of his faith and courage, he had plunged into the darkest thicket of heathenism, hewed out there a clearing, and planted a garden of God. Now the wilderness and the solitary place were glad for him, he had made the desert to rejoice and blossom as the rose.

His own dominating thought has ever been that God's guiding hand is signally manifest in the history of the Livingstonia Mission. As he wrote in 1900, "Alike in the time and circumstances of its inception, through the years of preparation and seed sowing, on to the whitening of the fields and the beginning of a harvest full of bountiful promise, the goodness and mercy of the Lord has been manifested. So to Him we ascribe all the honour, glory, dominion and power, acknowledging Him as the source of all the blessing in which we now rejoice, while with humble gratitude we praise Him for the redemption He has brought to many, and is still bringing to other, tribes of that so long benighted land."

IX: *The Legacies of War*

When the world war broke out Livingstonia was immediately in the thick of it. The operations of the Mission touched the hinterland of German East Africa along the whole frontier from Karonga to Mwenzo. Indeed, before Germany thrust herself into that region of Africa, the Mission occupied a station at Malindu, which was abandoned when it was found to have come under German rule. The drawing of the frontier was a bitter disappointment to all who had, up till then, been labouring for the good of Nyasaland, for it cut through the middle of tribes, and tore away populous districts whose sympathies were all with Britain, as represented by Livingstonia and the African Lakes Corporation. Even on this remote frontier Germany was prepared for war. Mwenzo had to be abandoned, and Karonga was only saved after a stiff fight.

The war inevitably disorganised the whole work of the Mission. Many of the teachers and people acted as carriers to the British forces, in which service thousands laid down their lives. When millions fell in the world war it was natural that no record should be kept of natives who died beside their loads on nameless forest paths, but their loyalty to the Empire should never be forgotten. Some of the medical missionaries were drafted into the Army Medical Service, others were put in charge of native transport. The Institution proved of inestimable value as a base of supplies to the troops operating from Karonga. Its post office was the point of departure for the despatch riders, its hospital was available for the wounded, and its meal mill was kept running day and night. No doubt these things were only a by-product, but it is worthy of note that all the money ever spent on the Institution was repaid tenfold in these terrible days of the world's need.

The war bequeathed to Livingstonia a twofold legacy. On the one hand, a heart-breaking legacy of sin and moral confusion. Especially at Karonga the presence of white troops demoralised the people to such a degree that a report went round the villages that even Dr. Laws had given up the Christian faith and advised them all to return to heathenism.

"How do you account for this?" said the missionary to his native elders as they sat together and wept over a shattered communion roll.

And the elders answered, "You warned us against the sin of drunkenness, but we never knew what drunkenness was till these white men came. You taught us to reverence the Sabbath, but they laughed it to scorn." And they went on thus through the ten commandments till the missionary was filled with a burning shame for his own countrymen who had struck so dastardly a blow to the Kingdom of God.

The other legacy is an open door of service to the north. A fertile and populous country round the north end of Lake Nyasa is now incorporated in the

Empire. The missions there are derelict, and it has fallen to Livingstonia to take their place and occupy the territory, for it seems unlikely that any German mission will again consent, even if allowed, to work under the British flag. This opens a vast new outlook. If the site of the Institution had a fault it was that it lay too near the north end of the field occupied by the Mission. Extensive tracts of what was German East Africa are nearer to the Institution than is South Ngoniland. Now the war has brought about the possibility of making the Institution central, and of building up around it a strong supporting Church without which it can never fully serve its purpose.

To this great new task the veteran Dr. Laws has girded himself with faith undimmed and a vision that moves out in ever widening circles towards the new heavens and the new earth. Of his own future, if he ever thinks at all, it would only be to repeat the words, written forty years ago in the first dark days of the Mission. "Here I must ever be fighting, working, watching, waiting, praying; rest and peace are the enjoyment, the heritage, of the land beyond."

CHAPTER VII

MACKAY OF UGANDA

I : *Stanley's Letter*

On November 15, 1875, a remarkable letter appeared in the *Daily Telegraph*. It had been written by Stanley in Uganda and entrusted to a young Belgian who was·to travel home down the Nile. The Belgian, however, was murdered by natives, and the letter, which was found afterwards on his dead body, came into the hands of General Gordon of Khartoum, by whom it was forwarded to England. It contained a stirring appeal to the Church to evangelise Uganda.

The situation was in the highest degree interesting and romantic. Less than twenty years before, that vast inland sea, the Victoria Nyanza, had been discovered, with the Nile pouring out at its northern end. On the northwestern shore lay the territory of Uganda, which in comparison with the savage tribes of Central Africa seemed to have made considerable progress in civilisation. It possessed roads and bridges, an army and a fleet of canoes on the Lake. Decent clothing was worn by the people, who showed some skill in agriculture, building and iron work. The King, an absolute monarch, ruled the land with the aid of his chiefs and high officials. Stanley speaks of Uganda as "the Pearl of Africa." At the time of his visit Mtesa the King, a man of intelligence, showed some interest in the Christian faith and expressed a desire that teachers should be sent out from England to Uganda. Hence Stanley's letter.

It was a challenge that could not fail to be taken up. It fired men's imagination to think that, when at last the ancient Nile had yielded up the secret of its birth, there should be discovered near its source a kingdom more civilised than any other in Central Africa whose king, prematurely described as "an enlightened monarch," seemed to be stretching out his hands to God. The Church Missionary Society promptly responded, and within six months of the publication of Stanley's letter a well-equipped party of eight missionaries left England for Uganda. Of these, the youngest but one, and, as the event proved, the most famous, was Alexander Mackay.

II: *A Missionary Engineer*

Mackay was the son of the Free Church minister of Rhynie in Aberdeenshire, and was born on October 13, 1849. His father, who was a man of wide learning, personally supervised the education of his boy, hoping one day to see him a minister. This idea, however, was not quite to the lad's mind. He had a passion for mechanics, and along with that a sense of the romance of missions. On the long Sunday evenings in winter, when his father was holding service in some remote part of the parish, he never wearied of hearing his mother tell of Carey and Martyn, of Moffat and Livingstone. How to combine these diverse interests, in mechanics and missions, was the problem that began to occupy his thoughts. It was considered as prophetic of his subsequent career that when quite a child he used to go among the masons who were building the Free Church of Rhynie, and when they jocularly asked him, "Weel, laddie, gaen to gie's a sermon the day?" he would reply, "Please give me trowel, can preach and build same time."

Mackay's family having removed to Edinburgh in 1867, he entered Moray House, the Free Church Training College for teachers, and completed the two years' course under Dr. Maurice Paterson. Thereafter, while maintaining himself by teaching in George Watson's College, he made a thorough study of engineering, both theoretical and practical. In 1873 he went to Germany to study the language and perfect his knowledge of engineering. For over two years he worked in Berlin and made many friends among the evangelical Christians of the city.

Meantime the idea of going to Africa as an engineer missionary had taken definite shape in his mind, and he had some correspondence with Dr. Duff and others on the subject. His proposal was something of a novelty, but was essentially sound. The value of medical science as an aid to mission work had come to be recognised, and Mackay claimed that a knowledge of the mechanical arts might equally become a handmaid of the Gospel. Christian civilisation, including all the wonders of modern science, was a unity, which should be brought to bear, in its full weight, on the heathen mind. It was while revolving these things in his mind that he saw the appeal of the Church Missionary Society for pioneers for Uganda, and, as there appeared no immediate prospect of an opening in connection with his own Church, he volunteered and was accepted.

The Committee of the Society held a farewell meeting on April 25, 1876, and at that meeting Mackay made some very memorable remarks. Speaking last he said, "There is one thing which my brethren have not said, and which I wish to say. I want to remind the Committee that within six months they will probably hear that one of us is dead." These words, spoken by a slim, blue-eyed boy, were startling, and there was a silence in the room that might be felt. Then he went on, "Yes, is it at all likely that eight Englishmen should start for Central Africa and all be alive six months after? One of us at least—it may be I—will surely fall before that. But," he added, "what I want to say is this. When that news comes, do not be cast down, but send some one else immediately to take the vacant place."

In less than two years we find him writing mournfully, "There were eight of us sent out. Only two remain. Poor Africa! When will it be Christianised at this rate?" Of the six who had fallen, two had died, two were murdered, and two invalided home. Mackay himself was the last survivor of the band, and was enabled to give fourteen years of unbroken service in Central Africa ere he was laid in his grave beside the great Nyanza.

III : *"Poor Moses"*

It was determined that the expedition should approach Uganda from the east coast opposite Zanzibar, travelling up through the country which shortly afterwards became German East Africa. This involved an overland journey of 800 miles to the south end of Lake Victoria Nyanza. It was an undertaking of no small difficulty, not merely to make the journey, but to carry all the equipment necessary for the founding of the Mission, including a boat for service on the Lake. Mackay was in command of the rearguard of 200 carriers laden with the boat and the heavier baggage. He encountered all the vexations, delays, and unforeseen troubles which are inevitable in African travel.

"It occurs to me often as a poser," he writes, "if two hundred men on the march can give such endless trouble, what anxiety must poor Moses have been in on his march with more than two million souls? The Lord God was with him, seems to be the only explanation, and my fears are all calmed by the fact that this caravan is the Lord's, and He will give all necessary grace for guiding it."

Several of the party were down with fever, and Mackay himself at last became so ill that he had to return to the coast. Having speedily recovered his health, he received instructions from the Committee in March, 1877, not to start for Uganda till the rainy season was over, but to employ himself meantime in making a wagon road from the coast to Mpwapwa, 230 miles inland. This work he successfully accomplished in the summer of 1877, bridging the nullahs, and cutting his way in places through the densest bush. He writes, "Imagine a forest of lofty, slender trees, with a cop between of thorny creepers, so dense below that a cat could scarcely creep along and branched and intertwined above like green, unravelled hemp. The line of the *road* through it is a path wriggling left and right, as if it had followed the trail of a reptile, and almost losing itself here and there, where the creeping wild vine and thorny acacia have encroached upon it. . . . Now the densest jungle has yielded to the slashing strokes of a score of Snider sword bayonets, which I have given my best men to carry."

His next instruction was to arrange for wagon transport along the road. This was no light task, for not only the oxen but also the drivers had to be trained. In spite of these difficulties Mackay was successful in bringing his loads on to Mpwapwa, but he found that the natives of the interior viewed with great suspicion the long train of oxen on the white man's road. Accordingly, having arranged for the loads to be brought on by carriers, he pushed forward rapidly to the Lake.

IV : *Into the Lion's Mouth*

Meantime his comrades of the pioneer party had been sadly reduced. They reached the south end of the Lake, but within six weeks Dr. Smith, Mackay's great friend and fellow-countryman, was dead. Shortly afterwards, two others, Shergold Smith and

O'Neill, having gone to the island of Ukerewe, were murdered in trying to shelter an Arab trader who had provoked the chief. Only one of the party had reached Uganda.

Mackay, in his own straightforward and fearless way, determined to visit Ukerewe at once, and if possible establish friendly relations with the chief, for he saw that the island commanded the approach to Uganda across the Lake. He felt, indeed, that he was putting his head into the lion's mouth, and the natives warned him that he would never leave the island alive. He went, however, in spite of these warnings, alone and unarmed. He remarks casually that he put some sulphate of zinc in his pocket, "in case I should require an emetic, Ikonge, the chief, being known as a poisoner!" His courage and frankness completely won the heart of the chief, who after a few days slew a goat in solemn pledge of blood-brotherhood.

Returning to the mainland he set to work to fit up the boat which had been brought from the coast. The Mission stores were in a state of absolute chaos. "Piled in heaps promiscuously lay boiler shells and books, cowrie shells and candle moulds, papers and piston rods, steam pipes and stationery, printers types and tent poles, carbolic acid, cartridges, and chloroform, saws and garden seeds, travelling trunks and toys, tins of bacon and bags of clothes, pumps and ploughs, portable forges and boiler fittings—here a cylinder, there its sole plate, here a crank shaft, there an eccentric. Despair might well be found written on my features as I sat down after my two years' march, to rest and look round on the terrible arrangement." Ten days' hard work altered the scene. "The engines of our steamer now stand complete to the last screw, the boiler is ready to be riveted, tools and types have separate boxes, and rust and dust are thrown out of doors. It seems to me more than a miracle how much remains entire of the really admirable outfit which the able Directors of the Society supplied us with when we left England."

He found the natives friendly and filled with a never ending wonder at the marvellous things he did. "When they see the turning lathe at work, or find me melting down the fat of an ox and turning out beautiful candles, their wonder knows no bounds. Again and again I have heard the remark that white men came from heaven. Then I teach this and that more intelligent fellow the use of various things, and try to impress upon all a truth I find them very slow to believe—that they themselves can easily learn to know everything that white men know. . . . Round comes Sunday, when tools are dropped, and the reason asked, 'Why.' I have my Bible, and tell that it is God's book, and He commanded the day of rest. Many know a little of Swahili which is, in fact, closely allied to their own language, and in that tongue I find many an opportunity to teach the simplest truths of religion, especially how God has come down among men. This 'great mystery of godliness' is the astounding story to them, and many I find eager to learn to read that they may know the book which I say God Himself wrote for men."

V: *For the Soul of a King*

After two months of this work the boat was ready and Mackay sailed across the Lake to Uganda, which he reached on November 1, 1878. Here he received a warm welcome from Mtesa, the King, who assured him of his friendship for England, and of his magnanimous resolve never to make war on that country! He fully believed himself to be the greatest monarch on earth, but though gifted with considerable intelligence, he proved in the end to be a sensual and capricious tyrant. For a time the omens were most· favourable. The King, his chiefs and people were greatly impressed by Mackay's mechanical skill, so far surpassing anything they had ever seen. "Truly," they said, "Mackay is the great spirit." All the more readily they listened to him while he tried to teach them the wonders of science and the greater wonders of grace. "God has blessed, and is still blessing, our work here," he writes, "for he has made the King and people willing at least to be taught. Fortunately Swahili is widely understood, and I am pretty much at home in that tongue, while I have many portions of the Old and New Testament in Swahili. I am thus able to read frequently to the King and the whole court the Word of God, and there is a mighty power in that alone. On Sundays I hold regularly divine service in court, and all join as far as they understand. Stanley began the good work, and now we are enabled to carry it on."

On Christmas Day he held a special service, when all the chiefs were in full dress and he explained the significance of the day. An Arab trader having just arrived with guns and cloth which he would sell only for slaves, Mackay vigorously opposed him. He spoke of the marvels of the human body and asked why such an organism which no man could make should be sold for a rag of cloth which any man could make in a day. Early in 1879 a party arrived to reinforce the Mission, having travelled up the Nile. The work now went forward hopefully.

It was not long, however, before clouds began to darken the sky. In February a company of French priests appeared on the scene in Uganda, and commenced that course of aggression which was destined to bear such bitter fruit. It is difficult to speak with moderation of their policy and conduct. With all heathen Africa to Christianise, Rome seems to have deliberately chosen the policy of following and subverting Protestant Missions. No doubt in the case of Uganda there were political, as well as religious influences, at work. France, having interests in Egypt, coveted the head waters of the Nile, and was pushing in from the west coast. The French missionaries in Uganda, to say the least, sympathised with this aim. They secretly supplied arms to their followers, whom they taught to look to France as their friend. Even after Uganda became a British Protectorate the intrigue was carried on. The two Christian parties which arose in course of time were known as the Ba-Ingleza and the Ba-Fransa. The division, as Sir Frederick Lugard pointed out, was not a purely religious one, but was practically a division between those who obeyed the law and those who resisted it.

These things were as yet hidden in the future, but meantime the coming of the priests created a most difficult and trying situation. They refused to acknowledge the Protestant Mission as Christian, claiming for themselves an exclusive right to that name. Mtesa was flattered by the presence of white men at his court, and displayed a lively interest in the various religious views which were pressed upon him. He seemed never to weary of question and argument. Moreover, as if to complete the religious confusion, the Arab traders in Uganda were advocating the claims of Islam, and had won a party to their side. The whole situation was strange and probably unique,—a heathen King in Central Africa with Mohammedan, Romanist and Protestant competing for his suffrage. The strongest argument of the Arabs was that the white men would come and "eat up the country." They told the King how a steamer was now on Lake Nyasa, and slave raiding was killed in that region. This was a consideration which Mtesa could fully appreciate, for the slave trade was one of his most profitable activities.

As weeks passed and the discussion still went on, it became increasingly apparent that the King, for all his keenness and intellectual interest, was morally a trifler. He delighted to play off one party against another, but from first to last he remained a heathen. One day, in a moment of unusual candour, he summed up the position thus. "If we accept the white men's religion, we must then have only one wife each, while if we accept the religion of the Arabs, we cannot eat every kind of flesh."

All through the year 1880 Mackay bore the strain of this conflict, sometimes with brightening hope, sometimes utterly cast down. On the 23rd of December, after describing the departure of two plundering armies, he writes, "This is the fifth time in the course of two years that a great army has been sent by Mtesa into Busoga, not to war, but avowedly to devastate and murder, and bring back the spoil—women, children, cattle and goats. The crime is awful. The most heart-rending of Livingstone's narratives of the slave hunts by Arabs and Portuguese on the Nyasa and Tanganyika shores, dwindle into insignificance compared with the organised and unceasing slave-hunts carried on by this 'enlightened monarch and Christian king.' We feel sorely downcast. Our last hopes seem gone. The lads who had learned the most, and seemed most impressed, have been put out of the way. The few chiefs of whom we had hopes have gone back, while the other chiefs and the King seem only daily to become more hardened and hopelessly sunk in every form of vice and villany. But is any case too hard for the Lord?"

VI: *"Great News"*

In March, 1881, three Baganda envoys, whom Mtesa had sent to England eighteen months before, returned home. They had seen the glories of England and been graciously received in audience by Queen Victoria, and it was hoped that their return would bring an influence favourable to the Mission. This hope, however, proved vain. The envoys had many wonders to tell, of seas and ships and cities. "We have no country at all," they said. But they immediately resumed their heathen life, and one of them showed himself a bitter enemy of the Mission.

About the same time a plague broke out in Uganda. Many died and the people became panic-stricken. Mackay, having no knowledge of the nature of the disease, refused to prescribe for it, but he urged upon the King the enforcement of sanitary precautions which did something to hinder the spread of the trouble. The Arabs had increased in their hostility towards Mackay and they brought the most atrocious charges against him, declaring that he was a criminal lunatic who had escaped justice in his own country and was plotting fresh crimes in Uganda. It suited the humour of the King to give ear to these charges, but he well knew them to be false, and besides he thought Mackay far too clever and useful a man to be driven out of the country.

Meantime Mackay went on steadily with the work. His barter goods were all either spent or stolen, and he must needs keep his forge going to earn his daily bread. But he began to gather round him an increasing band of disciples. Some would stand beside him at the bench while they recited their reading lesson, and when small portions of Scripture were printed in the language of Uganda they were eagerly bought up. One day in October, 1881, a slave brought a letter which he had laboriously written with a home-made pen and ink of soot. It ran thus. "Bwana Mackay, Sembera has come with compliments and to give you great news. Will you baptise him, because he believes the words of Jesus Christ?" It was "great news" indeed, for Sembera was a man of intelligence and exemplary life, and he became the first fruits of the Gospel in Uganda.

The following Christmas Mackay records a touching story of a boy who, after being under instruction for some time, took ill and died. Finding the end near he asked a heathen lad to sprinkle water on his head and name over him the names of the Father, Son and Holy Ghost. "I do believe," Mackay concludes with conviction, "that this baptism by a heathen lad has been written in heaven." On March 18, 1882, the first five converts were baptised, and thus was constituted the native Christian Church of Uganda which was destined so soon to pass through the fires of persecution to a glorious victory.

VII : *A Royal Funeral*

The life of a pioneer missionary is full of the strangest vicissitudes and most extraordinary experiences. Within a week the King's mother died, and he determined to give her a burial of unusual splendour. Having learnt that the great ones in England bury their dead encased in three coffins, he was not to be outdone. Could Mackay make three coffins? Yes, if the material was supplied. It proved, however, a bigger job than Mackay had bargained for and cost him a month's hard work. Everything had to be on the biggest possible scale. A small army of native smiths and labourers was commandeered, trees were cut down and dragged in from the forest, while copper trays, drums, and vessels of every sort were hammered out to make the metal shell. After infinite trouble the three monstrous boxes were finished, the outermost "with strong ribs like a schooner and looking like a small house rather than a coffn." The body of the old queen was enclosed, packed in valuable cloths, and the whole was finally deposited in a huge pit thirty feet deep, which was filled with cloths and covered up. Mackay estimated,—and the Arabs by an independent calculation reached the same figure,—that £15,000 worth of cloth was buried in the grave.

The fame of these obsequies resounded through the land and gave Mackay a unique reputation among the people. One happy result flowed from it. Walukaga, the King's head blacksmith, was brought under the influence of Mackay and listened eagerly to the Gospel. By and by he became a Christian and a leading member of the Church.

Mtesa was ill of a tedious disease, and in his trouble he turned to the heathen witchdoctors. They recommended that human sacrifices on a large scale should be offered upon all the surrounding hills. This atrocious order was promptly carried out. Executioners lay in ambush along the highways leading to the capital and seized all passers-by. A chief or a rich man might ransom himself, but for a poor man there was no escape. When a sufficient number of victims was collected they were all slaughtered on the appointed day. In 1884 Mtesa died as he had lived, a heathen. Mackay's services were again in request to make the King's coffins. On this occasion two sufficed of more moderate dimensions.

VIII : *Mwanga the Persecutor*

The new King was Mwanga, a lad of seventeen, who had been on friendly terms with the Mission and promised to show it every favour. Like more august monarchs, however, when he came to the throne he forgot his promises. It soon became apparent that things had taken a decided turn for the worse. Mwanga was weak and vain, as well as vicious, and accordingly he began to display his power and to play the part of the haughty tyrant. He flung himself with zest into every heathen abomination, and because the Mission condemned these he became a bitter enemy and a persecutor.

On June 30, 1885, he set the crown of martyrdom on the heads of three native Christian lads. Mackay and his colleague, Mr. Ashe, were going down to the Lake accompanied by two of their boys when they were suddenly set upon and driven back home with violence, while the two boys were arrested. That night the Mission house was searched, but fortunately the Christians had gone into hiding. Next morning Mackay heard that the two lads, together with a third, had been burnt to death. It was said that in the fire they sang a hymn in the language of Uganda, "Daily, daily sing His praises." "Our hearts are breaking," Mackay writes. "All our Christians dispersed. We are lonely and deserted, sad and sick."

Mwanga, shortly after, sent for Mackay and pretended that the execution had been carried out without his knowledge. No doubt some of his principal chiefs were more bitterly hostile than the poor weakling of a King himself, who was swayed to and fro by his passions and fears. He now adopted an attitude of more friendliness, deposed seventeen heathen chiefs and put others, friendly to the Mission, in their place. Mackay writes, "The King has saved himself and us by this sharp stroke. God be thanked." Mwanga was now receiving Christian instruction, and things began again to look hopeful.

In the autumn, however, there occurred a tragic event which clouded all the brightness. This was the murder of Bishop Hannington and his party on the borders of Uganda. The story is one of the most familiar in missionary annals. Early in the year Hannington had been appointed the first bishop of East Africa, and after some time spent at the coast he set out for Uganda. Instead of journeying to the south end of the Lake as the pioneer party had done, he chose a route much farther to the north, and travelled inland from Mombasa through the country now traversed by the Uganda railway. This route was shorter and healthier than the other, and gave direct access to Uganda round the north end of the Lake. Unfortunately the Bishop was ignorant of the state of feeling in Uganda. The Arabs had never ceased to affirm that the white men would come to eat up the country, and this had recently been confirmed by German annexations at the coast. The King and his chiefs felt comparatively safe behind the great barrier of the Lake, but they believed that real danger would arise when white men approached the country by the north end of the Lake, where it lay most exposed towards the coast.

It was this very route that Bishop Hannington had unhappily chosen. When the report of his advance reached Uganda there was a great stir at the court and consternation at the Mission. Mackay sent the boat across to the northeast corner of the Lake in an endeavour to intercept the Bishop, but without avail. Unconscious of all this, the caravan from the coast moved forward till near the borders of Uganda. The Bishop, leaving the main body, pushed on more rapidly with fifty carriers, and approached the point where the Victoria Nile flows out of the Lake. Here the whole party were made prisoners, and after a week of suspense came the order for their execution. Hannington met his death like a brave man and a Christian, bidding his murderers tell the King that he died for the Baganda.

The news of this catastrophe soon reached the mission. Mackay heard the whole story from eye-witnesses, and fortunately recovered Hannington's private diary, which he sent home. But no word was spoken openly about the murder as Mwanga denied all knowledge of it and became very threatening. His favourite page, having ventured to say that it was wrong to kill the white man, was by the King's instant order taken out and burnt to death.

Of this sorrowful time Mackay writes, "We had been enjoying much blessing in our work, and many more have been baptised. Now no one is allowed to come near us under pain of death. Yet they do come, chiefly at night. Mwanga would be glad to be rid of us, yet he will not let us go, all of us at any rate, as he means to keep us as hostages, because he dreads punishment. At the same time he threatens to put us in the stocks, and challenges England and the whole of Europe to release us."

Yet not for a moment did the great missionary cease from his work, as the following brief entry shows, "Writing out revision of St. Matthew's Gospel. Ashe busy setting it up. Time of persecution has always been a printing time." He also arranged that the Christians should meet in small companies at the houses of the native elders, and thus they would be trained to rely upon their own resources.

Meantime things went ill with Mwanga. His eyes gave him trouble, then his store of powder blew up, killing a number of the people and burning down his house. He took refuge in the house of his Katikiro, or Prime Minister, but next day it was struck with lightning and another explosion took place. Mwanga was now certain that the missionaries had bewitched him, and he vowed vengeance. He was a contemptible creature, a poor besotted drunkard, brandishing a knife and boasting what he would do, but unfortunately for the country he was King, and the lives of millions were in his hands.

The storm burst at the end of May, 1886, when an order was given for the arrest of all the Christians. Eleven were killed the first day and a systematic hunt was begun in all directions. Of the murders, mutilations and tortures that followed there is no complete record, save in the books of God. But the bitterness of the persecution may be judged from the fact that in one day thirty-two Christians, including many of the leaders of the Church, were slowly burnt to death. These martyrs made a noble end, so that the head executioner, like the centurion at the Cross, was compelled to bear witness, reporting to the King that "he had never killed such brave people before, that they died calling upon God."

It will not surprise those acquainted with Church history that this persecution, instead of dismaying the Christians, inspired them with new faith and courage. Many seemed utterly fearless, and even rash. Others, who had made no confession previously, now came forward desiring baptism. Mr. Ashe tells the story of one, named Kiobe, who had asked for baptism. " 'Do you know what you are asking?' I said to him. 'I know, my friend,' he replied. 'But,' I said, 'you know if you say you are a Christian they will kill you.' 'I know, my friend.' 'But,' I said, 'suppose people asked you if you were a reader, would you tell a lie and deny it and say no?' 'I shall confess, my friend,' he replied. Mackay and I both thought him worthy of the rite. So he was baptised there and then."

IX: *"The Universe is God's"*

As the persecution continued the two missionaries thought it might ease the situation for their converts, and lessen the King's dread of the white man if they left the country for a time and went to the south end of the Lake. Mackay, however, had been putting forth all his mechanical skill to win the favour of Mwanga and his chiefs. Accordingly he was considered too useful a man to be allowed out of the country, but permission was at length given to Mr. Ashe to leave. After his departure in August, 1886, Mackay was alone in

Uganda for a year. It was a year of hard work and great anxiety. "I am plodding on, teaching, translating, printing, doctoring, and carpentering. . . . Praise God! St. Matthew's Gospel is now published complete in Luganda, and rapidly being bought. I merely stitch it, with title-page, and supply loose cover. Binding, by and by. This work, with the packing and giving medicine to the Christians ordered off to war, and sitting up to all hours, teaching households, has thoroughly exhausted me. I am almost entirely broken down with fatigue and anxiety and want of sleep." Again he writes, "What sadness and melancholy comes over me at times, and I find myself shedding tears like a child! Then those wonderfully consoling psalms of David and Asaph, which send a thrill of joy through my whole being. This all but omnipotent reign of evil weighs one down, and then the exultant hope of its eternal destruction, and the ultimate triumph of good, cheers me up to more endurance, and perseverance to the end."

The hostility of the Arabs increased, and their cry about the white men eating up the country became more incessant. Stanley was now approaching Uganda from the Sudan, and it was said that if once he and Mackay met it would mean the ruin of the country. The French Fathers, also, who were playing a deep game of their own, encouraged this idea. "The King himself said that had the Arabs told him 'not to let Stanley and Mackay meet,' he would have looked on their words as merely enmity, but when a *white* man said this, it must be true."

In the circumstances Mackay felt compelled to press

for leave to depart. Fortunately, at this juncture, a missionary called Cyril Gordon arrived at the south end of the Lake. Mwanga, who was familiar with the renowned General Gordon of Khartoum, took a fancy to having a missionary of that name in his country. So it was agreed that Mackay should cross the Lake, and Gordon come to take his place. He left Uganda in July, 1887.

Mackay, about this time, was earnestly pressing the condition of Uganda upon the attention of the Church at home. He saw that European control of some kind was inevitable, but he had little hope of the development of the country and the prosperity of the Mission unless a railway were built from the east coast to the Lake. He speaks of it as the one sure means of "breaking the backbone of native cantankerousness." He had no interest in the expansion of Empire, and he was no advocate of armed intervention, but his heart bled for the sufferings of the Christians of Uganda, and the more widespread horrors of the slave trade. Why, he asked, should Christendom stand by and see Christians slaughtered? Why should England supply the guns and powder that made the slave-raider irresistible? It seemed to him no sufficient reply to say that the African was only suffering what the early Christians had suffered, and that he must work out his own salvation. As well might one argue that he must be left alone to invent his own steam engine, and painfully build up his own civilisation, instead of being led by a shorter road and taught to profit by the experience of other nations.

Mackay was well aware of the difficulties of the

problem, but like other missionaries he welcomed the appearance of civilised government in Africa in the interest of the common people of the land. Writing to his colleague, Mr. Ashe, who had gone to England to inform and rouse public opinion, he says, "To relieve men from the wrongs under which they perish, to secure freedom for the oppressed, yet not by 'blood and iron,' is a crux indeed for statesmanship. We want not so much an arm of flesh but heads of wisdom, human hearts, and helping hands. There is no need for gunpowder, that remedy is even worse than the disease. . . . This African problem *must be solved,* and in God's name it shall be solved, for God means it to be solved. It is not for the sake of the few scattered and despised missionaries that we are determined that this end shall be attained, but for the sake of Africa itself. Brutality must cease in God's universe, for the universe is God's, not the devil's. . . . The chronic bloodshed and cruelty, practised in inner Africa, cannot be ended by gunboats catching prizes on the ocean. What is that but plugging up the aperture that the pus may find no exit, while all the time we are destroying the blood by daily administering a deadly poison,—arms and ammunition, support and countenance, to Mwanga and other butchers of our black brothers? The rights of poor men, who wish to live lives of peace, are more divine than are the rights of royal robbers and murderers."

X: *"The Best Missionary Since Livingstone"*

Mackay now settled at Usambiro at the south end of the Lake, where he set to work to organise a mission station, in preparation for the arrival of Parker, the new Bishop, who was expected soon with reinforcements. The party arrived, and for a short time Mackay, so long a solitary, enjoyed the delight of Christian fellowship. But very soon Bishop Parker and Blackburn, one of his companions, died, Walker crossed the Lake to join Gordon in Uganda, another was invalided home, and Mackay was once more alone.

Meantime there was serious trouble in Uganda. Mohammedan and Christian chiefs united to expel Mwanga, who had plotted a wholesale massacre. Then the Mohammedans, by a sudden coup d'état, overthrew the Christian party and wrecked the Mission. Within a year the Christians had made terms with Mwanga, and restored him to his throne, as they vainly hoped, a humbler and a wiser man. In August, 1889, Mackay had the pleasure of welcoming Stanley on his return from the relief of Emin Pasha in the southern Sudan. They were three weeks together at Usambiro, and Stanley, who had long been familiar with Mackay's work, wrote of him with the warmest admiration as "the best missionary since Livingstone." "I was ushered in," he says, "to the room of a substantial clay structure, the walls about two feet thick, evenly plastered, and garnished with missionary pictures and placards. There were four separate ranges of shelves filled with choice, useful books. *'Allah ho Akbar,'* replied Hassan, his Zanzibari head-man to me, 'books! Mackay has thousands of books, in the dining room, bedroom, church, everywhere. Books! ah, loads upon loads of them!' . . . He has no time to fret and groan and weep, and God knows, if ever man had reason to think of 'graves and worms and oblivion,' and to be doleful and lonely and sad, Mackay had, when, after murdering his bishop, and burning his pupils, and strangling his converts, and clubbing to death his dark friends, Mwanga turned his eye of death on him. And yet the little man met it with calm blue eyes that never winked. To see one man of this kind, working day by day for twelve years bravely, and without a syllable of complaint or a moan amid the 'wilderness,' and to hear him lead his little flock to show forth God's loving kindness in the morning, and His faithfulness every night, is worth going a long journey for the moral courage and contentment that one derives from it. . . . Like Livingstone he declined to return, though I strongly urged him to accompany us to the coast." Stanley's company passed on their way homeward, leaving "that lonely figure standing on the brow of the hill, waving farewell to us."

The next visitor to Usambiro was Bishop Tucker, but there was no Mackay to welcome him. Stanley was not alone in urging Mackay to come home. The Directors of the Society and his friends pressed upon him to take his furlough, but he would not quit his post till reinforcements should arrive. He sent home an urgent appeal for "a strong batch of good men," saying that the Continental idea of "every man a soldier," is the true watchword for Christian missions. Ere the reinforcements arrived his own call had come. After a brief, sharp attack of fever he died on February 8, 1890. His last work was the translation into Luganda of the fourteenth chapter of John's Gospel—the story of the many mansions of the Father's house. Then from his fourteen years of exile he went home.

Six months later Bishop Tucker arrived at Usambiro, and thus describes the scene. "The Mission station, having been the work of Mackay, was of course well built. There was the Mission house—there the workshops—over there the printing house, and away yonder the cattle kraal. To see Mackay's tools lying idle and rusting in the workshops—the forge with its dead embers, the lathe motionless—was a pathetic and touching sight. But still more touching was it to wend one's way to the little burial place some distance off, and to stand by the graveside of the three who lay there—Mackay, Parker, and Blackburn." . . . "The loss of Mackay," he concludes, "was the heaviest blow that had yet fallen on the Mission. His faith, his courage, his intellectual capacity, his untiring industry, combined to form one of the most remarkable characters of the age in which he lived. It will be long ere the impress which he left on the lives and characters of the Baganda will be effaced. It will be longer still ere his noble example of devotion to the highest ideals, of courage in the face of almost insurmountable difficulties, of self-sacrifice and self-denial, ceases to inspire men to a participation in the noblest of noble enterprises,—the bringing to a saving knowledge of the truth those who sit in darkness and the shadow of death."

CHAPTER VIII

GRENFELL OF THE CONGO

George Grenfell was one of those who were drawn to the Dark Continent by the immortal story of Livingstone, and like his hero, besides being a great missionary, he attained to the front rank as an explorer. The mighty Congo, father of African rivers, and second only to the Amazon among the rivers of the world, drains the whole country from the Great Lakes to the Atlantic and from the Sudan to the Zambesi. Its tributaries would dwarf the rivers of other lands, and they join with the main stream to form a magnificent network of waterways in the very heart of the Continent. For a quarter of a century Grenfell moved along these waterways in his little steamer, the *Peace,* ever seeking to win an entrance for the Gospel into savage hearts, ever ambitious of bearing the good news to more distant tribes, and, ere he finished his course, he had the joy of being welcomed with Christian hymns in places where once he had been met with showers of poisoned arrows.

I : *From Cornwall to the Cameroons*

Grenfell was born on August 21, 1849, at the village of Sancreed in Cornwall, and was the son of a country carpenter. Those who are disposed may find ample evidence in his career of the proverbial doggedness of the Cornishman. His family, however, removed to Birmingham when he was only three years old, and that city became his home till he reached manhood.

It is remarkable how trivial an event may determine the course of a human life. A curious instance of this is found in the spiritual history of Grenfell. His family belonged to the Church of England and he was sent to St. Matthew's Sunday School along with his younger brother. There happened, however, to be a boy at the school who bullied them, and to escape from him Grenfell and his brother left, and went to a Sunday School connected with Heneage Street Baptist Church. This Church was henceforward his spiritual home, and at the age of fifteen he was received into its fellowship by baptism.

Regarding the beginnings of his spiritual life he afterwards wrote, "My earliest religious impressions of a serious kind date back to the early sixties, when the great wave of awakening that followed the revival of '59 was passing over the country. My interest in Africa began even earlier, being aroused by the pictures in Livingstone's first book, and deepened when I was about ten years of age by the reading of the book itself. Among the earliest of my resolves as a Christian was that of devoting myself to work in Africa, and, though I cannot claim that it never wavered, it was certainly ever after my dominant desire."

On leaving school he entered a warehouse, where he showed considerable aptitude for business, and came in time to have very excellent prospects. But his interests were centred in church and mission work. He belonged to a band of strenuous young men, connected with Heneage Street Church, whose Sunday, beginning with a prayer meeting at seven o'clock in the morning, included about seven services, with tract distribution in the intervals, and who rose on Monday morning like giants refreshed to attend a class in elementary Greek at the minister's house at half past six! They formed a Theological Class, and invited the Roman Catholic bishop to appoint some competent person "to discuss with us in a calm and friendly spirit the points upon which we vary in belief." On the bishop failing to reply Grenfell was instructed to write a letter of expostulation. Their energies found a more profitable outlet in publishing a little quarterly magazine, called *Mission Work*, the object of which was to set before its readers "proofs from all quarters of the globe that the Gospel is, as of old, the power of God unto salvation."

In September, 1873, Grenfell gave up business and entered the Baptist College, Bristol, to study with a view to becoming a missionary. As was to be expected he did not find student life altogether to his taste, but his character and missionary enthusiasm made a lasting impression upon the men of the College. After his death a fellow-student wrote of him, "Grenfell and I were in the same year, though he was very considerably my senior. I looked up to him with a great deal of respect, and loved him right away. Everybody loved him. He was strong as a lion, gentle as a woman, intensely sympathetic and absolutely devoted. There were missionary students who changed their minds. Grenfell's mind was fixed. Africa was in his brain and upon his heart."

After a year's training Grenfell was accepted by the Baptist Missionary Society for service in Africa. The veteran missionary, Alfred Saker, was at home on furlough from the Cameroons, and it was arranged that Grenfell should accompany him on his return. They sailed from Liverpool the week before Christmas, 1874, and reached the Cameroons in the following January.

The Cameroons Mission, like the Presbyterian Mission in Calabar, had its birth in the West Indies. The plantation slaves who for generations had been swept away from the shores of the Gulf of Guinea longed to carry the Gospel back to their homeland. In 1840 two Baptist missionaries from Jamaica settled on the island of Fernando Po, which lies in the inmost recess of the Gulf of Guinea, about four degrees north of the Equator. In 1844 they were joined by Saker, who began work on the mainland and during thirty years of heroic service laid the foundations of a Christian community.

In the Cameroons Grenfell served an apprenticeship of three years during which he was being prepared for his great work on the Congo. His station was at King Akwa's Town, on the south bank of the Cameroons River, about twenty miles from the sea-coast. Here he made acquaintance with that pitiful mixture of savagery and civilisation so characteristic of the West coast of Africa—kings dressed like dignified scarecrows, chiefs who would cringe for a bit of tobacco, men rejoicing in such names as Brass Pan, Pocket, and Liverpool Joss, women with a dozen brooches fastened in their hair for lack of a dress to pin them to. And combined with all this, as if to prevent the onlooker from regarding it lightly as mere pantomime, there was stark naked heathenism with its superstitions, its cruelties, its hopelessness.

Early in 1876 Grenfell was married, but in less than a year his wife died, and he tasted the first deep sorrow of his life. Fortunately he was joined about this time by Mr. Comber who became his dearest friend and fellow worker for the next ten years, till he also fell a victim to the deadly climate of the West Coast.

With the instincts of a pioneer Grenfell was assiduously plying his canoe along the various waterways, seeking to win the confidence of the people. He found many of their villages unpleasantly inaccessible. Some were buried in deep swamps, others were perched on rocky hills, these sites having been chosen for refuge in the old slave raiding days. Very soon he became convinced of the advantage of pushing on into the interior. For reasons both of health and of efficiency it was desirable to get away from the swampy coastland with all its corrupting influences. "In all my journeyings," he writes, "I have kept in view the object of finding the best route into the interior, for I believe that if the same amount of effort which is bestowed here were bestowed upon some inland station it would produce far greater results. . . . It would be a grand thing to be able to push away right beyond the influences that operate so adversely, and it can be done. . . . It is cheering to one who longs to get inland to know that the sympathy of the Society runs in that direction too."

Ere he could give effect to these ideas in the Cameroons he was called away to service in a vastly bigger field.

II: *The Giant Congo*

Six hundred miles south of the Cameroons the Congo enters the Atlantic. Although the mouth of this giant river was discovered by the Portuguese in the 15th century little or nothing was known of its course. A hundred miles from the sea, navigation was barred by a region of cataracts, beyond which the map was blank. In 1877 all this was changed. Stanley took up the problem of the African waterways where Livingstone left it. Setting out from the east coast he passed beyond Lake Tanganyika and struck the Lualaba at Nyangwe. From there he followed the course of the river northwards to Stanley Falls, and then westwards till he appeared at the Congo mouth. Among other important discoveries he showed that, beyond the region of cataracts, there was a thousand miles of magnificent waterway to the Stanley Falls, above which the river was again navigable southwards to Nyangwe. All along the course of the river great tributaries gave access to the country for hundreds of miles on either bank. The vast extent of this river system may be indicated by saying that if it were superimposed upon the map of Europe it would cover the whole area from the Shetland Isles to Smyrna, and from Moscow to the Pyrenees. At last Equatorial Africa lay open from the west coast, and drew the eager eyes of explorers and traders, of missionary societies both Protestant and Romanist, and, alas, also of the devil in the shape of King Leopold of Belgium.

The Baptist Missionary Society had for some time been considering the feasibility of work on the Congo, and upon Stanley's discoveries becoming known a prominent supporter of the Society, Mr. Arthrington, immediately offered £1000 to start the mission, and expressed the hope "that soon we shall have a steamer on the Congo, if it be found requisite, and carry the Gospel eastwards, and north and south of the river, as the way may open, as far as Nyangwe." Thus encouraged the Society instructed Grenfell and Comber to proceed to the Congo and break new ground. The feelings with which Grenfell received these instructions may be given in his own words to the Committee. "The decision of the Committee to undertake this new effort we feel to be the right one, and pray most earnestly that it may prove to be so. God seems to hold out far more glorious prospects of success there than appear to be possible here. The difficulties there may, indeed, appear less because they are farther off than those by which we are surrounded here. However, if I stayed here I should never give up trying to open a way for the Gospel, and though the difficulties there may, on a closer acquaintance, prove even greater than those at Cameroons, I shall still try, for the victory is sure."

In July, 1878, the pioneer party landed at the Congo mouth, where they were cordially received by a Dutch trading house, and shortly after they proceeded up the river in their own boat. They were welcomed at San Salvador by the King of Kongo, but were unable to reach the upper river owing to the determined hostility of the natives who wounded Comber so that he narrowly escaped with his life. Next year, however, reinforcements arrived from England, and by following a route along the north bank of the river they succeeded in reaching Stanley Pool, immediately above the cataracts. The road to the upper river being now open, a steel boat was sent out for the use of the Mission, and Mr. Arthrington offered money to build a small steamer. "I believe the time is come," wrote that generous and farseeing man, "when we should make every necessary preparation to carry out the original purpose of the Congo Mission—to place a steamer on the Congo River, where we can sail north-eastward into the heart of Africa for many hundred miles uninterruptedly, and bring the glad tidings of the everlasting Gospel to thousands of human beings who now are ignorant of the way of life and immortality. I have therefore, now to offer to your Society one thousand pounds towards the purchase of a steamer of the best make and capacity, and its conveyance and launch on the river at Stanley Pool, and three thousand pounds for the perpetual maintenance of such steamer on the Congo and its affluents, until Christ and his salvation shall be known all along the Congo, from Stanley Pool to the equatorial cataracts."

III: *Pioneering in the Peace*

The result of this was the building of the mission steamer, the *Peace,* which will ever be associated with the name of Grenfell. "For months, which added up to years, she was the home of his wife and babes, who accompanied him in his eventful voyaging. Her plates and rivets were as dear to him as his own skin, and the throb of her engines was like the beating of his own heart. Her missionary honour was to him a thing beyond price, and when the State seized her for purposes alien to her holy work, his grief was passionate, as though the ship had a character to be blasted, and a soul to be stained."

The *Peace* was a little screw steamer, drawing twelve inches of water, and constructed in sections to enable her to be taken to pieces for transport over the cataracts. During 1882 Grenfell was at home superintending the construction of the steamer. By December the work was finished and he sailed from Liverpool with his precious freight, accompanied by a young missionary engineer. On coming home to England Grenfell, who had remarried in 1879, left his wife on the Congo where she was now waiting his return with a baby whom he had never seen. He reached the mission station of Underhill at the foot of the cataracts only just in time to see his baby die. The young engineer also died not long after, and Grenfell was left with the whole responsibility of the steamer on his shoulders. The task of transporting it beyond the cataracts was no light one. Each load had to be carried through two hundred miles of difficult country, covered with long grass and cut up with ravines across which the packages had to be slung by ropes and pulleys. After months of labour and anxiety the loads were brought safely through to Stanley Pool.

These early days of the mission were heavy with many sorrows. The good seed was sown in tears, while man after man fell from the ranks. Grenfell was almost in despair. "Single-handed, as four of our stations are at this moment, who can be surprised at disasters? . . . If more men don't soon come, the Congo Mission will collapse, and the work that has cost so much will be thrown away."

Cheered by the news that two engineers were on the way out, Grenfell resolved to leave the building of the *Peace* to their skilled hands, and meantime to explore the course of the river in the steel boat. Accordingly he voyaged for three weeks up the south bank, and then, crossing the river, returned along the north bank. He found the natives timid and suspicious but generally friendly. He was amused by the antics of a medicine man who, on the approach of a storm, forbade the rain to fall, and kept on forbidding it throughout the course of a two hours' downpour at the end of which he claimed the victory. But everywhere sad evidences were seen of the unhappy condition of the people.

Grenfell writes, "How much this part of Africa stands in need of help I cannot tell you, words seem utterly inadequate. I cannot write you a tithe of the woes that have come under my notice, and have made my heart bleed as I have voyaged along. Cruelty, sin, and slavery seem to be as millstones around the necks of the people, dragging them down into a sea of sorrows. Never have I felt more sympathy than now I feel for these poor brethren of ours, and never have I prayed more earnestly than now I pray that God will speedily make manifest to them that light which is the light of life, even Jesus Christ, our living Lord."

On his return from this trip Grenfell was met with

sad news. Two of the mission staff were dead, both the engineers had died on the way out, and his father also was dead. "But we have not lost heart," he writes. "We cannot but believe that more help will be speedily forthcoming. Such trials do not kill the faith nor quench the ardour of Christians."

He now felt that he must himself undertake the building of the *Peace*. With such help as was available he successfully accomplished the work. "She lives, she lives," cried the natives when they saw the steamer move in the water. The missionaries were no less enthusiastic. "You will have heard," wrote Comber, "how good God has been to us, especially in the matter of the steamer—how dear old Grenfell has alone accomplished the gigantic task of reconstructing her. I can tell you we are proud of Grenfell, and thankful to God for him." Grenfell himself said he thought that the *Peace* had been "prayed together."

The maiden voyage of the *Peace* was a complete success. Grenfell and Comber steamed on her half way up to Stanley Falls, turning aside to explore several of the chief tributaries. In travelling thus among strange and savage tribes they found themselves time and again in positions of peril, and Grenfell complains of the physical effort required to keep on smiling when things might be on the brink of tragedy. It was heart-breaking to encounter ever fresh examples of an almost incredible ingenuity in wickedness. But over against that was the joy of "taking *for the first time* the light of life into those regions of darkness, cruelty, and death."

For the next year or two Grenfell led a wandering

life, plying his little steamer to and fro along the Congo waterways, and surveying the country in the interests of missionary advance. Not without many thrilling experiences. "Thank God we are safely back," he writes, at the end of one of these voyages. "It might have been otherwise, for we have encountered perils not a few. But the winds, which sometimes were simply terrific, and the rocks, which knocked three holes in the steamer when we were running away from cannibals, have not wrecked us. We have been attacked by natives about twenty different times, we have been stoned and shot at with arrows, and have been the mark for spears more than we can count." "The people are wild and treacherous, for several times, after a period of apparently amicable intercourse, without any other cause than their own sheer 'cussedness,' as the Yankees would say, they let fly their poisoned arrows at us."

At one place he encountered a tribe of friendly cannibals who offered him a wife in exchange for a fat boatman on whom they had fixed their longing eyes. At the Stanley Falls he met the notorious Tippoo Tib, mentioned by Stanley, who dominated the whole region west of Tanganyika and was raiding along the banks of the upper Congo. "We counted," he says, "twenty burned villages and thousands of fugitive canoes."

The geographical importance of Grenfell's work was immense. He traced the course of the Kasai River southeast towards the Zambesi. He ascended the great tributary, the Mubangi, northwards till it brought him to the Sudan, and he showed that at the great bend of the Congo the Aruwimi flows in from the east and opens a waterway almost to Uganda. These discoveries raised the inspiring hope that the various missionary forces working in from the east and west coasts might soon join hands across the continent.

IV: *The Belgian Octopus*

Forces of another sort, however, were at work. As early as 1883 Grenfell notes the high-handed policy of the Belgian Expedition. "They have been most unscrupulous, even in these days of small things—what will they be with the whole thing fully developed?" Alas, how little did the Christian word imagine whereunto this thing would grow! Two years later, on his return from an up-river voyage, Grenfell was staggered by a letter from the Administrator intimating that all his maps and observations belonged to the Government, and rebuking his presumption in sending them home to the Baptist Missionary Society. With restrained indignation he replies, "Your intimation that in the British Colonies subjects are not free to go where they will, and that the State has a 'right to possess itself of the fruit of a civilian's labours,' comes upon me as a great surprise."

But the Belgian octopus had fastened on the Congo, and Europe tamely suffered King Leopold to assert the monstrous doctrine that this vast region was his private property, and all its inhabitants his slaves. How charmed at first were the natives to discover that the juice of the rubber vine had a value in the white man's eyes, and could enable them to buy the glittering trinkets on which their hearts were set! How soon, with spirits crushed by forced labour, floggings, imprisonments, mutilations and murders, they pronounced their verdict of despair, "Rubber is death." These things were as yet hidden in the future.

The year 1887 was memorable in the annals of the Mission as "the Black Year," when six of the missionaries died in seven months. Grenfell was at home on furlough, but on hearing of the first four deaths he hastened his return to the field, although his health was precarious. On reaching the Congo he was met with the news of two more deaths. Friends of the Mission at home were stunned by these losses, and spoke of withdrawing from so deadly a field. But Grenfell was resolute. "We can't continue as we are," he wrote. "It is either *advance or retreat*. But if you retreat, you must not count on me. I will be no party to it, and you will have to do without me. I might plead with the Churches that for the sake of our great Head, for the sake of the terrible sin-stricken 'heart of Africa,' that out of love for and regard to the memory of our dear Comber, who died just a year ago, that for each and all of these reasons they should keep their pledges, but my heart is hot within me, and I feel I cannot plead. If love and duty and sacred promises are nothing, nothing that I can say will avail."

Faith triumphed, and in the next three years the blanks were filled and three new stations were established on the upper river. Grenfell settled at Bolobo, some distance above Stanley Pool, and it continued to be his home for sixteen years. He describes the place as "a sort of bottle neck" on the river, but at the said bottle neck the Congo is two miles wide, and can be called narrow only as compared with its width above and below, where it expands to six or seven miles.

In these days Grenfell was much alone, at his station or voyaging in the *Peace*. "Eh, Tom, lad," he exclaims in a letter to an old friend, "it is a shrivelling-up sort of work, so much alone, and surrounded by so much sorrow and sin." Yet he loves the solitude, for he finds that he has greater liberty in talking to the people when there are "no critical whites about." He has leisure for many long thoughts. "There is nothing like work in the Mission field," he writes, "for widening one's horizon. Where I am exactly, I don't know, any more than a good many celebrities seem to know where they are. I know John 3:16, and that's good enough holding-ground for my anchor. As you say, Christianity wants more of Christ's Spirit and less Theology. So say I, my dear Tom. Our Christianity is too much a matter of words, and far too little a matter of works. One might think that works were of the Devil, by the assiduity with which the great proportion of our Church members keep clear of them."

Wrestling with the difficulties of translation he can find no word in the language to express the idea of forgiveness. Unhappy Congo, where no one has ever known what it was to forgive or be forgiven! Yet the work is not without encouragement. In 1889 he records, "At Bolobo, on the first Sunday in March, I held the first Baptismal Service on the upper Congo, and on Sunday last I opened the first meeting house. Being Easter Day we had a talk about the Resurrection, and altogether a very enjoyable service. About seventy natives were present."

In 1890 the Belgian authorities, in spite of vigorous protests by the Mission, commandeered the *Peace* for their own use. Grenfell was profoundly moved. "They are taking my heart's blood in taking the *Peace*," he said. "The best thing that could happen to the poor *Peace*, would be for her to run on a rock, and sink. She will be no more the old *Peace*, when they have done with her. The soul has gone out of her!" Then, starting to his feet, he exclaimed, "I go to England to agitate." He went to England, and so effectually did he agitate that the Belgian authorities were fain to climb down with the best grace they could, and the *Peace* was restored to her owners. The King of the Belgians, perhaps by way of atonement, conferred on Grenfell at a personal interview the insignia of "Chevalier of the Order of Leopold." Grenfell humorously described himself as feeling "like a barn door with a brass knocker," but the day came when he publicly declared that he could no longer wear the insignia with honour.

V: *Sorrows Public and Private*

In 1891, with the consent of the Mission, Grenfell was appointed Commissioner to settle the southern boundary of the Congo Free State. This work, which involved six months of hard travel through difficult and unknown country, he completed to the satisfaction of the authorities, neither he nor the Mission being a penny the richer by it.

On returning to Bolobo in September, 1892, his first task was to build the new mission steamer, the *Goodwill,* which he had brought out from England a year before, and had expected would by this time have been afloat. Then the *Peace* was so badly worn that she had to be half rebuilt. Always the Mission was short-handed through illness and death of workers. Often Grenfell was alone in charge of the two steamers, and the big forward movement on which his heart was set was continually delayed. Yet the work made progress. A printing press was established at Bolobo, and the Church there steadily increased. Grenfell describes the happy time he had with his boys and girls at the Christmas of 1894, with "a leg of buffalo in the nick of time for roast beef," and a famous tug of war, ending in a broken rope and a sudden jumble of legs and arms. But he adds, "I've had anything but a Merry Christmas," and he goes on to speak of his many burdens, chiefly the conditions of the Bolobo people, their superstitions, lawlessness, witchcraft and quarrelling. "How it is these people have escaped the fate of the Kilkenny cats, I can't imagine. It can only be explained by the fact that they are always buying slaves, and that they have not always been so bloodthirsty as they are now. Poor Bolobo! I wish I could see more readiness to accept what they know and feel to be the Truth, which we try to explain to them. My heart is very, very sad at times, as I think of them heaping up judgment against themselves."

There are moments when he grows impatient at the sluggishness of the home Church. "I wish to goodness I could get our folk fervid enough to embark on some more or less 'madcap' scheme, such, for instance, as the redemption of the promises we made some eighteen or nineteen years ago, when we talked of Lake Albert and the Nile. . . . Don't think I've dropped pioneering because I'm tired of it. I never think of it but my soul burns to be up and off again." In 1896 he had the joy of planting a new station at Yakusu, near the Stanley Falls, and the remarkable success of this new mission was a great comfort to him amid the trials and sorrows of his later years.

The Congo atrocities were now being brought more and more fully to light. Into that tragic story it is impossible here to enter. Grenfell was slow to believe the worst. He clung to the hope that the excesses committed by local agents would be checked and punished by the Government, but at last he was compelled to realise the bitter truth. King Leopold, that arch-hypocrite, had scattered his myrmidons over the Congo with orders to get rubber at whatever cost, and, while professing to spend thousands in philanthropic efforts to uplift Central Africa, he was drawing in millions saturated with African blood.

The missionaries saw the tribes enslaved, tortured, mutilated, delivered over to the tender mercies of native soldiers, many of whom were cannibals, and all to provide dividends of a thousand per cent to the royal rubber company. What could they do but voice in the ears of humanity the bitter cry of a perishing people? This, of course, was mightily inconvenient to the authorities. So a Commission for the Protection of the Natives was appointed, and Grenfell and other missionaries were asked to serve on it. But the whole thing proved to be a blind, and Grenfell indignantly resigned. "You can easily imagine," he writes, "the Protestant missionary is not a popular man just now on the Congo." Every obstacle was thrown in the way of the Mission. Grenfell was informed that certain children must be taken away from his school and handed over to Roman Catholic missions, because "being a Roman Catholic State it had no power to place orphans under any other than Roman Catholic tutelage!" "It is very significant," Grenfell remarks, "that the way should be opened up for English Roman Catholics, and closed against us. Evangelical Christianity does not breed the dumb cattle beloved of officialdom."

In 1899 Grenfell suffered an irreparable loss in the death of his oldest daughter, Pattie, who had come out from England while yet in her teens to join the Mission. After a few months' work she was struck down with fever while voyaging with her father in the *Peace,* and only lived long enough to reach Bolobo and expire in her mother's arms. She was the fourth of their children to find a grave on the Congo. Next year Grenfell's own health gave way, and he had to come home to England. It seemed, indeed, as if his day was done, but he rallied, and November, 1891, saw him again on the Congo.

VI: *The Joy of Harvest*

His last term of service was deeply shadowed and saddened by the frightful sufferings of the natives under Belgian rule, and by the increasing hostility of the authorities who persistently refused to grant new sites to the Mission. Yet amid many sorrows he tasted of the sweet joys of harvest. In 1902 he writes, "You will be glad to know that here at Bolobo, shorthanded as we are, we are not without evidences of progress and blessing. People are more willing to hear, and give heed to the message they have so long slighted. In fact many are professing to have given their hearts to the Lord Jesus, and there are signs of good times coming." Again he writes, "Our services are crowded as they have never been before. Some are beginning to talk of building a bigger chapel. . . . God's Spirit is manifestly working among the people. We are all compelled to allow it is not our doing, but God's."

In his voyages, also, up the river, he sees many signs of happy change. Thus he writes of one place, "A few weeks more than twenty years have elapsed since I first landed at the foot of the same cliff, and was driven off at the point of the native spears. The reception was very different this time. The teacher and a little crowd of school children stood on the beach to welcome us, and I spent a very pleasant time in the village on the plateau just beyond." And again, "I shall never forget one evening, a few weeks ago, as we were looking for a good camping place among the reed-covered sandbanks, about half way between this and Yakusu. There was a threatening sunset, and we sought a shelter from what promised to be the stormy quarter. Then suddenly we heard strike up, 'All Hail the Power,' from on board one of the big fishing canoes among the reeds. We had not observed the canoe, but the crew had recognised the *Peace,* and gave us what was to me a glorious welcome which will long remain a blessed memory. Whose heart would not be moved to hear 'Crown Him Lord of All' under such circumstances? It was just about this same place that, twenty-one years ago, we came first into view of the burning villages of the big Arab slave-raid of 1884. I little thought to live to see so blessed a change, and my heart went forth in praise. Yes, God's Kingdom is surely coming."

Grenfell still had the ardent spirit of the pioneer, and retained in a wonderful degree his physical vigour. He explored the Aruwimi eastward to within eighty miles of Uganda. On another voyage he ascended above the Stanley Falls and followed the Lualaba southward to forty miles beyond Nyangwe. His great desire was to advance along the line of the Aruwimi, and join hands with the C.M.S. Mission in Uganda, but the Belgian authorities interposed wearisome delays until he was in despair.

At last, in October, 1905, permission was given to settle at Yalemba near the mouth of the Aruwimi, and Grenfell made haste to occupy the place. The voyage up river occupied six weeks, and after discharging his stores at Yalemba, he turned the steamer south to Yakusu, where his heart was much refreshed by the work of God. It had been agreed that one of the missionaries at Yakusu should become Grenfell's colleague at Yalemba, but he confessed that he dared not take any of them away from so great a work. So he returned to Yalemba alone.

VII: *"The Death of Tata Finished"*

But his strength was spent. After struggling on for several weeks against fever and increasing weakness he at last consented to seek help. His native boys gently carried him on board the *Peace* and steamed down the river to the nearest station at Bapoto. Here, in spite of every effort, he gradually sank. Near the end he looked up at the dark circle of sorrowing faces gathered round his bed, and said, "Help me, my children, I am dying. Pray for me." Then later he added, "Jesus is mine. God is mine."

He died on July 1st, 1906. One of his native boys, recording the simple story of his burial, concludes with exquisite beauty, "Then we sang another hymn. Last of all we closed the grave, replacing the earth. And so the death of *Tata* (Our father) finished." How fitly spoken! For Grenfell's place is among the living, not the dead. While strength endured he still advanced, leaving behind him the graves of his children, set like milestones along the Congo banks. His own is now the farthest. So he died. But the inspiration of his holy zeal, and of his love for Christ and Africa, remains a deathless thing.

CHAPTER IX

COILLARD OF THE ZAMBESI

"The banyan tree," wrote M. Coillard, "is the true emblem of the Church of God. Each one of its mighty branches bears roots, each root that touches the soil and grows there becomes a new trunk which in its own turn must spread its branches farther and strike new roots." It is no less a true emblem of his own life and work. Having struck his roots deep in Basutoland and guided the growth of the Church there for twenty years he became the pioneer of that Church's mission to Barotsiland and nourished the first upspringings of Christian life in the regions beyond the Upper Zambesi.

I: *A Son of the Huguenots*

François Coillard was born on July 17, 1834, at Asnieres-les-Bourges, a village in Central France. He came of peasant stock, and when only two years old, on the death of his father he was left with his mother in circumstances of deep poverty. The attachment between the widowed mother and her son was peculiarly warm and tender. The family belonged to the French Protestant Church and François was brought up in an atmosphere of warm evangelical piety and missionary enthusiasm. He never forgot the joy of his first missionary gift, consisting of money which he earned by gathering dung off the public road and selling it for a trifle to the schoolmaster. Yet his mother shrank from the thought of giving up her boy to the cause.

"Oh, mother," he said one day, "how splendid it must be to be a missionary."

"Yes, my child, it is a much finer thing than even to be a pastor."

"Why should not I become a missionary myself?"

"Oh, my child," exclaimed the fond mother in sudden alarm, "be anything else you like but not that. You would be lost to me."

Nevertheless the idea persisted, and after he passed through a crisis of conversion the impulse became irresistible. His mother's opposition was at length overcome, less by argument than by the influence of secret prayer. Rising in faith to accept the sacrifice, she wrote,

"My child, I understand now that God is calling you. Go, I will not keep you back. I had always hoped you would be the staff of my old age, but after all it was not for myself I reared you. And the good God will not forsake me if He sends you to the heathen."

He was accepted for training by the Paris Missionary Society and on the completion of his studies he was ordained at Paris in May, 1857. On that occasion he closed his address with these words, which finely express the spirit of the man:

"Pray for me that I may be faithful to my Master, faithful unto death. Pray, oh, pray, all and earnestly, that I may grow grey in His service, and that He may grant me the joy of seeing my ministry close only with my death." It was a prayer which was answered to the full.

II : *Life in Basutoland*

His destination was Basutoland, South Africa, where the Paris Missionary Society had carried on a mission since 1833. The Basutos, a powerful Bantu tribe, formed in those days an independent kingdom under their great chief, Moshesh. The strength of their kingdom lay in the mountainous region of the Drakensberg, west from Durban, where Natal borders on Cape Colony and the Orange Free State. So placed, it could not fail to be a storm centre in the days when Boer and Briton were contesting possession of the country and when tribal power was as yet unbroken.

On Coillard's arrival at Cape Town he found war raging in Basutoland. The Boers of the Orange Free State had invaded the territory and burnt some of the French Mission stations. On peace being restored the Mission was reorganised and the newly arrived missionary was sent to Leribé in the extreme north of Basutoland. The district was under the rule of Molapo, the ablest but most intractable of the sons of Moshesh. Moshesh himself, a man of intelligence and strong character, was deeply interested in Gospel truth and before his death made open profession of his faith. The case of Molapo his son was very different. Clever and well instructed in Bible truth, he had at one time made a Christian confession but was now a hopeless renegade. He seemed to have a double personality.

On Sunday he would exhort his people to be converted, while secretly he opposed and persecuted. In later life he became subject to fits of epilepsy and ended his days little better than a raging maniac.

Into such a situation the young and inexperienced missionary was thrown and left to his own resources. One of his colleagues wrote of him, "Few young missionaries have had a lonelier life or one of more entire self-sacrifice than his during the three years he passed there alone before Mme. Coillard came out to him, surrounded by an entirely heathen population, hearing nothing from morning till night and often all night through but the wild shouts, the din of their heathen dances, their drunken brawls. His food at that time consisted of native bread with thick milk and pumpkin. I remember him spending days knee deep in water, cutting the reeds with which to cover his first little cottage. At that time there was not a single Christian in the whole district with whom to hold Christian fellowship."

So unpromising was the field that the Conference of 1860 proposed to give up the station of Leribé. Coillard, however, was resolute. "Do they think I am made of wood, with a heart of stone? Do they not know that it is just *because* I have suffered at Leribé that my heart is so much attached to it?"

In February, 1861, he was married at Cape Town to Christina Mackintosh, who had come out from Scotland to join him. It was the fulfilment of a long deferred hope and the beginning of a perfect married life of thirty years. Mme. Coillard, the daughter of a Scottish minister, high spirited and fearless, sagacious and tactful, above all of an intensely religious and devoted spirit, became the never failing helper and solace of her husband, and the companion of all his wanderings till, worn with toil and travel, she was laid to rest under a lone tree beyond the Zambesi.

The work of the mission went forward prosperously and they had the joy of baptising their first converts. Owing to the hostility of the chief and other difficulties the building of a permanent house was at first impossible and for two years they made their home in the wagon and a tent. When at last a house of three rooms was finished Mme. Coillard "felt like a princess." They were not destined, however, to enjoy it long.

III: *War and Exile*

In 1864 war again broke out, Boer commandos raided the country, and the wildest disorder prevailed everywhere. Quarter was neither given nor received. Boer and Basuto shot each other at sight. For months the Coillards were isolated in a war-tortured country within sight of burning villages and bloodshed. Tying a white flag on the end of a long reed, M. Coillard started across country for the home mail which had not come to hand for six months. When about sixty miles from home he was struck down with fever and appeared to be dying. His wife, on hearing the news, immediately saddled a horse in spite of the entreaties of the terrified natives, who feared equally to accompany her or to be left behind unprotected. After a terrible night ride she reached her husband and nursed him back to health.

Barely had they returned home when the Government of the Orange Free State resolved to expel all missionaries from Basutoland. No reason was ever given for this act of oppression nor was any notice taken of the appeal of the missionaries for an inquiry. A commando appeared one day at Leribé to execute the order.

"Leave nothing behind," said the commandant, "for you will never come back here."

After a painful journey through the Drakensbergs the exiled missionaries reached Natal, where they lived for the next two years, and laboured among the Zulus. They also paid a visit to Dr. Moffat at Kuruman. Writing of this visit to his mother in France, M. Coillard says, "Do you remember the long evenings when I used to read to you Mr. Moffat's book about Africa while you stripped the hemp? Did you ever think then that I should come to Africa and that I should see Mr. Moffat and his station, Kuruman? The Lord's ways are wonderful."

IV: *Revival*

In 1869 Britain established a protectorate over Basutoland and the missionaries were enabled to return to their work. The Coillards found Leribé practically in ruins, but to their great joy the spiritual side of the work had suffered no loss. The troubles rising out of the war had led to a revival of religion among the Basutos. The paramount chief, Moshesh, who was dying, declared himself a Christian. Nathanael, his nephew, one of his trustiest counsellors and the bravest of his chiefs, who had long been a Christian at heart and a true friend of the Coillards, was baptised about this time.   In Europe the Franco-Prussian war was raging and Nathanael heard something of the anxieties and privations of M. Coillard's mother.   One day he brought an ox as a present for her, and, with it, a touching letter in which he said,

"My Mother, I am Nathanael Makotoko, I salute you in the love of the Lord.   Since the war has broken out in France my heart is full of sorrow.   I know what war is, what sufferings it brings.   I thought of you. . . . You think you have only one son in Leribé because you sent only one.   No, my Mother, you have two, the second is myself, Nathanael.   It is you who have given me life in the Lord, for it is you who gave birth to the servant of God, my beloved pastor, who came to draw me out of darkness.   You have many children in Leribé and you will have many more yet."   Surely these words must have brought to the aged mother's heart some foretaste of that "hundred-fold" which the Lord promised to those who have given up their dearest for His sake.

The power of the Gospel was felt even by the ignorant and the aged.   A poor old Matabele woman, a derelict from her tribe, was at first dull and listless. She could not pray, she said, for she did not know the Basuto language.   When she was told that she could pray just as well in her own tongue she exclaimed in amazement, "Do you really mean that God understands my language?"   When she was assured of this it opened all the floodgates of her pent-up heart.

"Perhaps you think I am old," she said.   "No, I

have grown a young girl since I began to serve Christ."

She spoke of her past life of heathenism and beer-drinking, but she added, "I did not know any better. I had not yet heard that I had a Father."

The most notable fruit of this revival was the birth of a missionary spirit among the Basuto Christians, and it was determined to break new ground in the Banyai country, immediately to the north of the Transvaal. A little band of Basuto evangelists was sent out but they were forced to return after having been imprisoned for some time in Pretoria. The Mission Council then resolved to ask M. Coillard to lead the expedition in person. The proposal came upon the Coillards like a thunderbolt, for they had all their preparations made for a well earned furlough in Europe, the first after twenty years of service. Nothing is more characteristic of them than the spirit in which they met this crisis.

V: *"With Such an Escort We Can Go Anywhere"*

M. Coillard wrote, "The thought of leading a wandering life full of perils and adventures, and leaving our station for so long, appalled us. However, we fixed a day for our final decision and redoubled the ardour of our prayers. The evening of this very day, our friend C——, who was not at all in sympathy with the appeal they had addressed to us, and who had not the least idea that the moment had come for us to decide, read the 91st Psalm to us. Never had it seemed so beautiful. When, after marking the magnificent promises, which came so aptly one by one, our brother came to verse eleven, 'He shall give His angels charge over thee,' the climax was reached. My wife and I looked at each other and understood. The moment we were alone, 'Well?' I said to her.

" 'With such an escort we can go anywhere,' she replied.

"We knelt down, our resolution was taken, peace and joy returned to our hearts."

Be it remembered, these were not youthful enthusiasts ready to dare anything in blind inexperience, they were veterans, spent with years of service, who were called to greater effort and costlier sacrifice. It was an act of supreme devotion to pluck up their home life by the roots and face, at their age, the hardships of pioneering.

In April 16, 1877, the expedition had an enthusiastic send-off. The young Basuto Church cherished the rosiest dreams of its success, but the leaders were under no delusion as to the task before them. As the wagon began to move Mme. Coillard turned to her husband and said, "We have weighed anchor, God knows where we shall land. But he knoweth my wanderings, my tears are in His book." As the event proved, almost ten years were to elapse ere, in God's providence, they had again a settled home. They had embarked on a vaster and not less perilous Odyssey than Homer's.

The story of the expedition forms an almost incredible tale of adventure and of toil. After getting clear of the Transvaal they had to cut a virgin path northwards towards Mashonaland. Their reception at the hands of the Banyai was very different from what they had been led to expect. The chiefs were hostile and the people pillaged their goods. Once, when the lumbering wagon stuck fast in a ravine, it seemed as if the whole party would be massacred on the spot. Round them surged a mob of savages, brandishing spears, howling threats, snatching at the goods on the wagon. Mme. Coillard deliberately sat down under a tree and began to sew, with an excited warrior whirling his axe over her head. Her husband meantime was imploring and restraining the Basutos who were for seizing their rifles, "to die like men." He knew that the first shot fired would be the signal of the end. At last the terrified oxen lurched forward and the mission party were snatched, as if by the very hand of God, from the jaws of death. Years after, when in a similar position of peril on the upper Zambesi, M. Coillard told the story to his trembling followers, and concluded, "Well, my friends, mark my words. It will be just the same here. Not a hair of our heads will fall to the ground." And so it proved in the issue.

It was at this time that Mme. Coillard was smitten with sunstroke, from the effects of which she never entirely recovered. When she regained consciousness she reproached herself for "the sting of my heart as I opened my eyes once more on the light of this world." She added, "I did not realise till then how very unutterably weary I had become." A band of Matabele warriors now appeared on the scene, before whom the Banyai grovelled in abject terror. Coillard then learned that Lobengula held the Banyai tribes in subjection and resented the mission entering his territory by a back door. The whole party were made prisoners and hurried westward to Bulawayo, which they hardly dared to hope they would leave alive. Fortunately their knowledge of Zulu enabled them to converse freely with Lobengula, and even to convince that bloodthirsty tyrant of the honesty of their intentions. After three anxious months of captivity they were sent out of Matabeleland by the southwest, and came into Khama's country where they were welcomed by that Christian chief and his people. The question of the future of the expedition now became pressing. It seemed as if no course was open but to return south to Basutoland, yet, on the other hand, M. Coillard felt that the finger of God pointed unmistakably to the far north. The circumstances were indeed remarkable. Many years before, a branch of the Basuto people had fought their way north, crossed the Zambesi, and established their sway over a wide region in its upper basin. They became known to the world as the Makololo, whom Livingstone found the dominant power on the upper Zambesi. Since his day their vassals, the Barotsi, had risen in revolt and exterminated them, but their name was still held in respect, and their language, Sesuto, was spoken throughout the country. Here surely was the predestined field for the missionary labours of the Basuto Church, a field where no new language had to be learned, no new translations to be made.

The difficulties in the way, however, were most formidable. The route to the Zambesi lay across the great Kalahari desert. A previous attempt to found a mission among the Makololo had failed disastrously. In response to Livingstone's appeal, Helmore and Price of the L.M.S. had led an expedition to the north, but almost all perished, possibly by poison, and the mission had to be abandoned. Since the revolt of the Barotsi the whole region of the upper Zambesi was reported to be the scene of constant warfare and bloodshed. Yet all this only made brighter, by contrast, the vision of faith. M. Coillard wrote in his journal, "How splendid will be the day, which I see already dawning, when all the tribes of Central Africa will know Jesus and sing His praises. It will be a sight for angels. The sacrifice of a life is a small thing to contribute to hasten that glorious day."

A start was made in June, 1878, and after a trek of two months Leshoma was reached, a point on the Zambesi some miles above the Victoria Falls. Leaving his wife at Leshoma, Coillard crossed and travelled up the river to Shesheke, the home of some powerful chiefs of the Barotsi. He opened communication with Lewanika, the King of the Barotsi, and requested permission to settle in his country. Lewanika, however, was engaged in a desperate struggle to maintain his throne and could give no definite answer.

Meantime the mission party suffered terribly from fever. Coillard himself lay between life and death. Khosana, one of the Basuto evangelists, died, and Eleazar, another of them, fell ill. At last a message arrived from Lewanika granting the desired permission. "God be praised," exclaimed Eleazar. "The door is open." Then, as he felt himself sinking, he added, "My grave will be the fingerpost of the mission."

"Do you regret having come?" asked M. Coillard sorrowfully.

"Oh, no," he replied, "I do not belong to myself.

It is to the Lord I belong. It is His business, not
mine."

So died "a sure counsellor and a precious friend," as
M. Coillard, not without good reason, calls him.

It now became necessary to return to Basutoland, to
organise and equip the Barotsi mission. The joy of
the home coming to Leribé was deeply shadowed by
sorrow. In the long two years' trek three of the four
Basuto evangelists had died. M. Coillard scarcely
knew how to meet their friends, but the aged father
of one of them grasped his hand and said, "My father,
do not grieve. I offered the Lord the best thing I had,
and He has accepted my sacrifice."

In December, 1879, the Coillards left for their long
delayed furlough in Europe. It proved one of their
most arduous campaigns. The funds of the Paris
Missionary Society were so depleted that the Committee could not face the opening of a new field. Thus
it fell entirely on M. Coillard to raise every penny of
the funds required for the Barotsi mission. The work
was hard and, to his sensitive nature, distasteful, yet
he carried it through with complete success, winning
the confidence of the Churches in France, England, and
Scotland by his invincible faith and the charm of his
personality.

Back in Basutoland in 1882 he encountered difficulties of another sort. War had broken out again. Leribé Mission Station had been plundered and the village burnt. Indeed in the whole district, with a population of 35,000, not a village was left standing. Even
after peace was restored it seemed hopeless to stir up
the scattered and impoverished Church to a fresh inter-

est in Barotsiland. "How can people go to the Zambesi," it was asked, "when there is so much to do in Basutoland?" Only the driving power of an unconquerable faith carried the mission forward. "A missionary enterprise," wrote M. Coillard at this time, "is not like a balloon, launched into the air amid admiring crowds and then left to take its chance.

> "But tasks in hours of insight willed
> Can be through days of gloom fulfilled."

VI: *Among the Barotsi*

At last preparations were completed and in January, 1884, the expedition left Leribé for the Zambesi. Accompanying the Coillards were their niece, Elise Coillard; M. Jeanmairet, a young Swiss missionary; two artisans, and four Basuto evangelists with their families. Passing north through Khama's country they found a message of welcome from Lewanika, but by the time they reached the Zambesi Lewanika was dethroned and civil war raging. A weary year of uncertainty followed. M. Coillard speaks of "an utter lassitude, both moral and physical. It seemed to us sometimes that the springs had been overstrained, and the very sources of life dried up." The passage of the Zambesi was at length safely accomplished and the missionary band advanced to Shesheke, only to find themselves in the midst of bloodshed and terror. The very first night after they crossed the river some fugitive women who clung to Mme. Coillard for refuge were dragged off and butchered.

Slavery, witchcraft and all the oppressive evils of

African heathenism prevailed in Barotsiland. Thieving seemed to be a universal vice. Recounting some of his losses, M. Coillard half humorously offers them as a proof that "we have made no mistake in bringing the Gospel to the Zambesi." This faith upheld him through everything. He had in fullest measure the mystic insight which discerns the hand of God in all events, even the most untoward. It was this which made him write, after seeing his wagon overturned at a ford and all his stores and books sunk in the water, "The one thing that shone out amid the tumult of my thoughts was a lively sense of God's goodness." Yet there were hours of gloom and of reaction. Thus he writes again: "Night fell. But a darkness deeper than that of night oppressed my spirit. I was seized with an awful and overpowering sense of helplessness, distress and mental anguish."

The station at Shesheke was barely established when M. Coillard left it in charge of M. Jeanmairet, who had now married Elise Coillard, and himself pushed on, far up the river to Sefule, near the King's capital of Lealuyi. It was one of the most toilsome of all his journeys, for it meant dragging the wagon through a wooded and waterlogged country infested with tsetse fly. Mme. Coillard joined him in January, 1887, and once again, after ten years of a wandering life, they were settled in what might be called a home. Here they set to work, with failing strength but with unflagging zeal and devotion, to reclaim the wilderness of heathenism around them. The physical conditions were new and more arduous than in Basutoland. The country was a vast and steaming flat, inundated for some months every year and always feverstricken, a country where travel was difficult and where strenuous exertion was impossible.

VII: *African Royalty*

Lewanika had by this time regained his throne and mercilessly slaughtered his enemies. On the whole he was favourable to the mission, though with variable moods and fits of suspicion. He sent some of his children to school, notably his son Litia, who now reigns as the first Christian King of Barotsiland. The character of Lewanika, his slow emergence out of savagery and his wavering approaches to the Christian faith, make an interesting study. Being told that God hates the shedding of blood, he one day sends a message that he will shed no more blood, and therefore, having captured some children of his enemies, he has only poisoned them. Later he sends a herald to the school to warn the pupils that all who play truant or do not learn their lessons will be throttled. Gradually he came to be on terms of intimacy with the Coillards whom he both loved and trusted. More and more he seemed to feel a sense of isolation from his own people and their ways. Sitting in the little mission house he said, "This is my home. I have twenty-one wives but no home!" Perhaps, had he felt himself strong enough to resist his chiefs, he might have made profession of the Christian faith. Who can tell?

The royal pupils in the school were at first a source of much annoyance. Their attendants procured food for them by the simple process of plundering the neighbouring villages, so that the people began to desert the locality. The Princess Mpololoa required three slaves to attend her, one to hold her book, one behind to lean against, and one in front to act as a writing desk! The dignity of these young savages was jealously guarded. A native having accidentally brushed against a little daughter of Lewanika was slain on the spot by the child's attendants. Such were the awful depths in which the first foundations of the Kingdom of God had to be laid.

No picture of court life in Barotsiland would be complete without mention of Lewanika's sister, Mokwae, who reigned as Queen in her own right. She was a stout, comical looking figure, but a most formidable personage. Her ninth husband followed everywhere at her heels submissively, with many a trembling thought, doubtless, of his unfortunate predecessors, none of whom had died a natural death. Mokwae had been known, in moments of passion, to seize a sword and sweep a man's head off at one blow. Yet with the eternal feminine in her savage breast. "What lovely eyes you have got," was her first greeting to M. Coillard. To his wife she expatiated on the glories of the wardrobe she possessed before the war, "a grey hat with green and red, and a long dress. All the King's wives had just the same, and really we looked just like men." These hats and dresses had perished, with much else, in the war, and Mme. Coillard was welcomed as a dressmaker and milliner!

In 1890 there occurred a momentous event in the history of Barotsiland. An envoy from the British South Africa Company arrived to negotiate a treaty with Lewanika. The King himself was favourable to British suzereignty, influenced doubtless by the experience of Khama, who sent a message, "I have tasted of a delicious dish and I share it with you." The matter was discussed in full council of the chiefs, and M. Coillard, while carefully disclaiming all personal interest, was able to give such explanations as led at length to the signing of the treaty. But for his presence the result would have been very different. Thus in great measure through his work and the influence of his character a kingdom as large as France was peacefully added to the Empire. To the Barotsi themselves it was an immense benefit that by his work of Christian education they were in some degree prepared to meet the incoming tide of the white man's civilisation.

VIII: *"That Delicious Rain"*

In 1891 Mme. Coillard died. The last years of her life had been a continual struggle against fever and increasing weakness. All her strength, to the last ounce, she gave to the work, devoting herself principally to the women and children. It was October and the rains had not yet come. The earth was red-hot and the air was stifling. The night before she died the rain broke.

"Place me at the window," she said, "to let me hear that delicious rain."

It was a touch of God's mercy at the last. And she had the greater privilege, too, of hearing the first showers of spiritual blessing. Often she had prayed, "Oh, that Thou wouldest rend the heavens and come down," but the spiritual firmament was as brass and the earth iron. The last year had been the hardest. "Never, during our thirty years together," wrote M. Coillard, "had we passed through so many sufferings and distresses. She often said, 'What a year! I wonder how it will all end.' Everything seemed against us, everything."

The Sunday before her death Mme. Coillard was able to attend a service at Lealuyi. Litia had just returned from a visit to Khama's country and he rose and declared himself a Christian. "My father," he said, beaming with joy, "I am no longer the Litia of former days. I am converted. I have found Jesus." While he spoke, Mokamba, a young man of the royal family, broke down and sobbed aloud. Mme. Coillard was deeply touched and thrilled with joy.

"A Morotsi weeping," she exclaimed, "and weeping for his sins. I thought a Morotsi had no tears to shed. It is a sight I would have travelled three hundred miles to see."

On Monday she said, "Take me back to Sefula. It is there I would die." Her last words to her husband were, "Do be in earnest, do." Well might he say of her that her life was an alabaster box of ointment, exceeding precious, which she broke and poured out upon the Saviour's feet.

IX: *The Wedge of the Gospel*

After the death of his wife M. Coillard felt himself a lonely and homeless man, yet twelve toilsome years were before him ere he reached his rest. In 1892 he moved the mission station to Leafuyi, and his influence over the King and his people steadily increased. "In spite of all our disasters," he wrote, "I have the profound conviction that we have already forced the wedge of the Gospel into the social system of this nation. It is for others to drive it home with redoubled blows, and this mighty paganism, solid and formidable as it appears, will break up, as it has done in all times and in all countries." The losses of the mission had indeed been grievous, and many graves had been dug beside the Zambesi, but undoubtedly the work was telling. The King appointed one of the converts to be the Gambella, or Prime Minister, expressly to lead his people along the path of reform. Slowly but surely the wedge was pushing home.

In 1895 M. Coillard undertook a long journey up the river to break ground among the new and unknown tribes. He travelled in canoes provided by Lewanika, and was accompanied by the Gambella and other converts. Something was done to allay the suspicion of hostile tribes and the homeward voyage down the river was gladdened by the work of grace among the boatmen. Returning to Lealuyi seriously ill M. Coillard was compelled to leave at once for South Africa, where a skilful operation was the means of restoring him to a measure of health.

From the Cape he came home on his second and last furlough. Once again, through two years of incessant travel, he charmed Europe and pressed upon the Protestant Churches the crying need of Central Africa. It was while he was home on this visit that he was found to have given anonymously all the money he possessed to the Zambesi Mission. His friends felt that he might well retire, but his own heart told him that work still waited him, and a grave, beside the Zambesi. "My heart is still young," he wrote, "but the old tent is wearing out. I should like to have wings, to travel about the country and publish the Good News."

Having raised funds and enlisted a band of volunteers he returned to Africa. There was time for a brief visit to his old home in Basutoland. The sadness of farewell was mixed with the joy of witnessing the amazing progress of the Basuto Church. He naturally saw in this "the seal of God placed upon the call we felt we had received to the Zambesi." In many respects a new day was dawning for Central Africa. The mission party travelled to Bulawayo by the Cape to Cairo Railway, where M. Coillard lunched at Government House on the very spot where Lobengula had held him a captive at his kraal.

Arrived at his field of labour he was at once plunged into a sea of troubles which made his closing years among the most trying and painful of his life. There were bad seasons and political complications in the country. In the mission, deaths of beloved friends and valued workers threatened for a time to bring the whole work to a standstill. In three years, out of twenty-four young recruits, eight had died and eleven had been invalided home. Only five remained in the field. But perhaps the bitterest trial of all was the disloyalty and opposition of some of his Basuto helpers who had gone over to the Ethiopian movement and resented, with childish petulance, all control. Nothing could have been more perfectly Christlike than the tender, fatherly spirit in which M. Coillard bore with them, and strove to win them back to reason and charity. It was due to this that the trouble was less acute and gave far less trouble than in most other African missions. Yet in secret his heart bled, and he marked his Bible at the pathetic text, "I have laboured in vain and spent my strength for nought and in vain."

An episode of a very different kind created about this time a universal interest in Barotsiland. It was no less an event than the visit of King Lewanika to England in 1902, to attend the coronation of King Edward.

"Will you not feel embarrassed at your first interview?" asked M. Coillard.

"Oh, no," replied Lewanika coolly, "when we Kings get together we always find plenty to talk about."

This visit made a profound impression on Lewanika and his people. The Gambella who accompanied him summed up his impressions of England in the striking words. "The great ones honoured us, the believers showed us affection, but the people of the world despised us because our skins were black."

King Lewanika himself, on the Sunday after his return, came to the mission service and made a remarkable speech to the people, in which he said: "I have two words; the first is, Praise God and bless Him. In spite of all your fears I have come back to you full of life and health. . . . It is God alone whom we must praise. Let us talk no more about our ancestors, they are no Gods. My second word is this, The

Gospel is everything. I have seen many things, and many wonderful things, but I have also seen one thing that I cannot keep silent about. It is that everywhere it is the Word of God that guides kings and their councils, which makes people intelligent through their schools, and gives them security and happiness. The missionaries told me all this but now I have seen it. Barotsi, let us come out of our darkness. Come and hear the teachings of the missionaries, send your children to school, that we too may become a nation."

Unfortunately the King did not follow up these noble words by any declaration of his own faith. On the contrary, shortly after, he went, from motives of public policy, and paid a ceremonial visit to the shrines of his ancestors. Nevertheless the change was almost incredible from the savage warrior of twenty years before to the far-travelled and experienced ruler who could utter these enlightened sentiments. The change in his country was no less profound, "peace and security instead of anarchy and bloodshed, slave-raiding and slave-trading abolished, infanticide, torture, trial by ordeal and by witchcraft abolished, and drunkenness at that time never seen; also, as an indirect result, a great territory opened to civilised government without the firing of a single shot."

X: *Rest*

M. Coillard died on May 27, 1904. He had once written to a friend, "My great, *great* desire is not to live a day longer than I can work," and in the end this wish was fulfilled. He was buried beside his wife under their favourite tree at Sefula, where they had often sat together and which they had marked out for their last resting place. Over the grave stands a marble cross with the words, "To live is Christ,"—a literally true description of those two heroic lives, made perfectly one by their earthly love and, still more, by their heavenly devotion. May we not add with equal truth, when we think of their manifold toils and wanderings, "to die, gain."

CHAPTER X

I: *An Extraordinary Factory Lassie*

Mary Slessor was a wayward and original genius, consecrated to the service of Christ. In Old Testament history cases occur where the Spirit of God comes mightily upon a man, sweeping him beyond himself, so that natural timidity and weakness are overcome, weariness is forgotten, and in a holy frenzy some great work of God is wrought. Some such influence is needed to explain the extraordinary career of Mary Slessor. A Scots lassie of strong sense and shrewdness, timid and shy yet full of fun, with a vast store of nervous energy liable to discharge itself fitfully in bursts of jollity and daftness, she was captured and possessed by the Divine Spirit, and irresistibly impelled to do the strange work she did. In speaking of her it is difficult to avoid the language of extravagance. She is entitled to a place in the front rank of the heroines of history, and if goodness be counted an essential element of true greatness, if eminence be reckoned by love and self-sacrifice, by years of endurance and suffering, by a life of sustained heroism and purest devotion, it will be found difficult, if not impossible, to name her equal.

Mary Slessor was born December 2, 1848, in the city of Aberdeen, and was the second of a family of seven children. From her earliest years the home was made miserable by the intemperance of her father, and was only saved from total wreck by the toil and patient goodness of her mother. When Mary was eight years old the family removed to Dundee, in the hope that away from his old companions the father might make a new start. Unhappily there was no improvement, and Mrs. Slessor had to go out to work in the factory to earn a scanty livelihood for her children. Mary was left in charge of the house, but at the age of eleven she also began work in the factory as a half-timer. In such a home the children, delicate and ill-fed, could not hope to thrive and ere long three of them died. The father's habits grew worse, and Saturday night was a night of terror, often spent by Mary in wandering miserably in the streets. At length he died and left the home saddened yet relieved of the strain of his presence.

Even in the darkest years, however, there was a sunnier side. The tenderest ties of affection bound the mother and her children together, and they shared the same warm Christian faith. Sunday was the happiest day of the week and few of their church friends suspected the secret tragedy of the home, so jealously was it guarded. Their interest in missions seems always to have been strong. Mary's favourite game was to teach an imaginary school of black children. Her elder brother Robert used to announce that he meant to be a missionary when he became a man, and when the boy died the thought took serious hold of his sister that she might one day go in his place to the foreign field.

Years were to elapse before that ambition was ful-filled. Like many other distinguished missionaries Mary Slessor served a full term of apprenticeship in mission work at home. She had always been a diligent scholar in Sunday School and Bible Class, and an eager reader of the best books she could lay hands on. It was no ordinary factory lassie who studied Milton's *Paradise Lost* and sat up half the night over *Sartor Resartus*. Wishart Church, to which Mary belonged, started a mission in one of the worst slums of Dundee and she volunteered her services as a worker. She was small and fragile but full of pluck, ready to do and dare anything for Christ's sake. The mission rooms were in sad disorder.

"We shall need a charwoman to give the place a thorough cleaning," said the superintendent.

"Nonsense," said Mary, "we will clean it ourselves."

"You ladies clean such a dirty hall!"

"Ladies!" laughed Mary. "We are no ladies; we are just ordinary working folk."

And next night she and another teacher were hard at it with pails and scrubbing brushes.

At first the mission workers had to encounter a certain amount of opposition and rough usage, especially when they attempted to hold open air meetings. One night Mary found herself suddenly surrounded by a band of rough lads who threatened to "do for her" unless she promised to desist.

"I won't," said Mary. "You can do what you like."

"All right, here goes," shouted the leader, and he produced a lump of lead attached to a cord and began to swing it threateningly round her head. She stood without winking while the lead swished past her brow. After a few tense moments the lad suddenly threw it away, exclaiming with honest admiration, "We can't force her, boys, she's game."

Never was a word more fitly spoken. Mary Slessor was what would now be called a good sport. She had more than a dash of that daredevil spirit which leaps up in the moment of peril, not fiercely but good humouredly. First and last and always she was "game." The lads became her devoted followers, and years after the leader sent her the photograph of himself with his wife and children in grateful remembrance of the turning point of his life.

Mary's methods with her class of boys were quite unconventional. On Saturday afternoon she would join them in long walks into the country and was foremost in any fun that was agoing. Sometimes an impish spirit of mischief seemed to take possession of her. Once when walking with a girl friend she knocked at some cottage doors and ran away. "Oh, Mary, I am shocked at you," said her friend. To which remonstrance Mary gaily replied:

> "A little nonsense now and then
> Is relished by the wisest men."

All the week she was hard at work in the factory. For years she had been the mainstay of the home, and this continued till she seemed to have settled down for life to the toilsome lot of a factory worker. It was not till her twenty-eighth year that the horizon widened and the romance of her African career began.

In 1874 the Christian world was profoundly moved by the news of Livingstone's death. It marked an epoch in modern missionary history. To Mary Slessor it brought an intense revival of her missionary dreams, and she reviewed the possibilities afresh. She felt the time had come when she could be spared from home. Besides, she hoped to be able to send home part of her salary. Before volunteering for service she asked her mother's consent. "My lassie," said her mother, "I'll willingly let you go. You'll make a fine missionary, and I'm sure God will be with you." Calabar was the mission field on which her heart was set, but in making her offer of service she expressed her willingness to go anywhere. To her great joy she was accepted for work in Calabar, and after some months of training in Edinburgh she sailed for the west coast of Africa on the 5th of August, 1876.

II : *In Dark Calabar*

Calabar, or Old Calabar as it was wont to be called, was a household word in the United Presbyterian Church. A certain member of that communion, dimly conscious of having heard the name from childhood, asked a collector incredulously, "Is the old beggar living yet?" Few were so ignorant of what the name signified, for throughout the Church there was a proud interest in Old Calabar as the Church's most difficult and most romantic mission field.

In the inmost recesses of the Gulf of Guinea, a hundred miles east of the Niger, the Cross River rolls its waters to the sea. The surrounding country is now included in the British colony of Southern Nigeria. It is the ancestral home of the Negro proper, and in the days when the slave traders swept the west coast of Africa, multitudes were torn away from these regions and shipped off to the plantations in the West Indies. It was among the children of these plantation slaves that the idea of the Calabar Mission first arose. The United Presbyterian Church had had a mission in Jamaica since 1824, and when the slaves were emancipated many of them turned their thoughts back to the old home of their people, and longed to carry thither the story of the Cross. In this desire their missionaries warmly sympathised, and one of them, Mr. Hope Waddell, went to Scotland to arouse the interest of the home Church. Having secured the necessary help, he sailed for Calabar in 1845, in his little brigantine, the *Warree*. After some months spent there, he took the *Warree* over to Jamaica, and brought thence an additional band of helpers.

The Cross River cannot compare in volume with those giants of Africa, the Nile, the Niger, the Congo or the Zambesi, yet its estuary gives a surprising impression of magnitude. For the first thirty miles it maintains a breadth of ten miles. Above that point, though the breadth is not diminished, the channel is filled with a labyrinth of islands. Beyond these islands the Calabar River comes in from the east, finding its way by various channels to the main stream. Near its mouth, on opposite banks and with an island between them, lie Duke Town and Creek Town. Here the mission was commenced. When the *Warree* first cast anchor, a few trading ships lay in the river for barter with the natives. No white trader was allowed to settle on shore, and few had any desire to do so, for the country was regarded as a white man's grave. "Kings" were plentiful in Calabar. Every town of any size had its king, some of whom were prosperous traders and men of influence, especially King Eyo Honesty of Creek Town. But for the most part they were raw savages who sustained their kingship with ridiculous solemnity, robed in a strip of yellow cotton and crowned with a battered pot-hat. The wealthier chiefs and traders had their houses packed full of sofas and mirrors and every variety of English furniture, which they knew not how to use.

This slight contact with civilisation had done nothing to banish the superstitions or mitigate the barbarous customs of heathenism. Belief in evil spirits was universal, witchcraft and the poison ordeal were practised everywhere. The towns on the river bank offered human sacrifices to the spirit of the river for the success of the fishing. When twin children were born they were, as quickly as possible, buried alive, and the unhappy mother killed or driven into the bush. At the death of a chief or any man of importance there was a cruel slaughter among his people. A huge cavern was dug for a grave, and into it the body of the chief was placed, resting on the bodies of four of his wives, bound hand and foot but *living*. Slaves were then brought to the grave-side, their heads struck off, and their bodies tumbled in till the grave was full, when all was covered over with earth and trampled down. To such hideous customs add the horrors of tribal wars, of slavery and slave-raiding, and there rises the picture of a land covered with gross darkness and full of the habitations of cruelty.

III : *"Blessed with an Efik Mouth"*

When Mary Slessor arrived in Calabar the Mission had been in existence for thirty years and considerable progress had been made in the district immediately around Duke Town and Creek Town as well as a few miles up the river, but the interior of the country had yet to be penetrated. Back in the depths of the primeval forest savage tribes, some of them cannibals, raided and fought and wallowed in the abysmal night of heathenism. Nowhere was the darkness of Africa more dense than in the hinterland of the West Coast.

At first Mary was charmed with the novelty and beauty of her surroundings. After the smoke of Dundee and the confinement of the factory she revelled in the glory of the sunshine and the luxuriance of the tropics. The deadly climate had not yet laid its hand on her, and she vented her wild spirits in climbing the biggest trees in the neighbourhood. She claimed in after years that she had climbed every respectable tree between Duke Town and Old Town. Her home was with "Mammy" and "Daddy" Anderson in their house on Mission Hill above Duke Town, a one time haunted spot thick strewn with the decaying bodies of the unburied dead, but now the headquarters of the Mission. Mammy Anderson was a bit of a disciplinarian, and evidently found her volatile young friend "a handful," as the Scots say. She threatened that those who did not come for meals at regular hours must go without. To Mary regularity was next to impossible, but she found that, when she transgressed the rule, bananas and biscuits were smuggled to her, while her dear old Mammy turned a blind eye.

Meantime, with all her quaint ways and oddities, Mary had plunged into the work heart and soul. She rapidly acquired the language, and seemed to steep herself in the native mind. The people began to say that she was "blessed with an Efik mouth." She visited in their homes and addressed little audiences wherever they could be found. Gradually the shuddering depths of heathenism were unveiled before her eyes, and stirred her soul with infinite yearning and pity. She did not escape her share of west coast fever, and by the end of a three years' strenuous apprenticeship she was thoroughly run down and homesick. "I want my home and my mother," she confessed.

A short furlough in Scotland restored her physical vigour and she returned to Calabar in 1880 with fresh ardour. To her delight she was given charge of the work in Old Town and was left free to follow her own methods. It was a strange situation for a Scots lassie to be left solitary in a West African town where the vilest heathenism had combined with gin and the slave trade to make a hell upon earth. Yet this isolation was entirely to her mind, for more reasons than one. She was sending home a large part of her meagre salary to her mother, and to enable her to do this she lived almost entirely on native food. But chiefly she welcomed the opportunity of living among the people till she became like one of themselves. This was the secret of the extraordinary influence she acquired.

She loved the Africans and never wearied of them, however grieved and sickened in soul she might be by their heathenish ways. Perhaps the iniquity that lay heaviest on her heart was the systematic murder of twin children. In the benighted minds of the natives the superstition was firmly rooted that, when twins were born, the father of one of them must be some evil spirit with whom the mother had formed an unnatural union. Both mother and children were regarded with the greatest horror. The woman was driven out of her village as an accursed being, the infants were made away with at once, being either buried alive or crushed into an earthen pot and flung into the bush. The Mission was always on the outlook for these little waifs and many of them were rescued. It was useless to restore them to their mother, for she also regarded them with aversion and would, if she got the chance, destroy them with her own hands. The infants of slave mothers who died were also often left to perish, and the callousness of the people in regard to child life was appalling.

Mary Slesser's mother-heart yearned over these tiny morsels of black humanity. She gathered them in with both arms and soon her house was full to overflowing. From first to last she saved in this way scores of children, some of whom grew up in her home to love and serve her like daughters. Other babies came into her hands too enfeebled to live. These, when they died, she dressed and buried with reverent care, while the natives watched her with stupid wonder, saying, "Why this fuss about a dead child? She can get hundreds more."

While carrying on her work in Old Town, Mary Slessor constantly heard the call of the unknown, and felt increasingly the fascination of the dark, untraversed hinterland. Hers was the restless spirit of the pioneer, ever reaching out eagerly to the regions beyond. She had now no family ties in the home land, for her mother and sister were both dead, and her heart was wholly given to Africa. To bury herself in its darkest depths, to labour for its uplifting, to live and die among its people, was her sole and consuming ambition. At length in 1886 the Mission Council agreed that she should go up country and break new ground in Okoyong, a district lying in the angle between the Calabar and Cross Rivers.

IV: *Settled Among Savages*

Okoyong was the home of a fierce and powerful tribe, supposed to be of Bantu origin, for they were of better physique, lighter in colour, and with finer features than the negro tribes around them. Appalling stories of their barbarism reached the coast. They were a tribe of head-hunters, with no central authority, but each village under its own petty chief, all armed and suspicious of one another, prone to drunkenness and bloody brawls in the intervals between more serious fighting.

It was not easy to secure the consent of these wild people to the settlement of a missionary among them. Several visits were paid to the district but without result. At length in the summer of 1888 Mary Slessor went up the river herself and, making her way to a village called Ekenge, she secured the consent of the chief, Edem, to the building of a mission house there. No doubt one influence leading to this was the strange friendship which sprang up at first sight between Mary and the chief's sister, Ma Eme. The latter, though she never became a Christian, remained a lifelong friend of the Mission, and often sent secret warning when any plot or savage project was on foot. Mary returned to Creek Town to prepare for a permanent settlement in Okoyong.

On the 3rd of August she set out on her great adventure. It was a dull grey morning with a thick drizzle of rain. A few friends gathered at the river bank to see her off. "I will always pray for you," said one, "but you are courting death." She stepped into the canoe with five native orphans who formed her household,—the eldest a boy of eleven, the youngest a baby in her arms,—the paddlers pushed off, and in a few minutes they had disappeared in the mist. It was dark before they reached the landing place for Ekenge, and the village itself was four miles back in the forest. Taking the baby in her arms and urging forward the now terrified and weeping children Mary struck out along the forest path, leaving the men to follow with the loads. On reaching the village she found it deserted on account of a funeral carnival in the next village. She got shelter in a hut and waited for the loads to arrive. By and by news reached her that the men were tired and refused to come on. Mary at once rose up, retraced the four miles of forest path, routed the men out of the canoe, rallied and scolded them, and brought them all on to Ekenge by midnight.

In after years the same resolute spirit, full of dash and fun, carried her through a hundred toils and perils where any other woman would have sunk down and failed.

She was not long in making herself at home. She superintended and helped with her own hands the building of a mud-walled house. She went about with bare feet and bare head, subsisted on native food, drank unfiltered water, slept on the ground, got drenched with rain, and in short did everything that would have killed any ordinary person. She had a wonderful way with the natives. Her perfect mastery of the language, her fearlessness and good humour made her pleadings irresistible. She would plunge into the thick of a drunken brawl and separate the combatants. Even when more serious fighting was afoot she often intervened with success. So extraordinary did her influence become that, whenever any trouble arose, the instant cry of the women was, "Run, Ma, run." And run she did, at any hour of the night or day. Sometimes, if the night alarm was urgent, she sped along the forest path, clad only in her night dress. "Of course," she would explain apologetically, "they were not to know but what it was court dress." Strangely enough, she continued through it all a naturally timid and shrinking woman, trembling in every limb and praying in agony as she ran. But her tears were overpowered and her sensitive spirit was swept onward by an irresistible passion of heavenly love.

She continued with ardour her work of saving twins and other outcast children. She had at all times a considerable family under her care, but no matter how numerous they might be there was ever room in her heart and home for more. Sometimes two or three tiny hammocks would be slung from the roof around her bed so that she could conveniently reach and rock the little sleepers through the night. Scenes were witnessed that would have moved a heart of stone. On one occasion, hearing of the birth of twins in a neighbouring village, Mary ran to the rescue, but ere she had gone far she met the unhappy mother staggering along the path, with the babies in a basket on her head and the whole village hounding her off into the forest with execrations. Mary took her home, and as the poor creature lay dying she cried out to her husband for forgiveness, sobbing in her delirium, "I did not mean to insult you."

On another occasion Mary heard some women remarking casually how strange it was that a baby should live five or six days in the bush. On inquiry she found that the baby of a dead slave mother had been cast out about a week before because nobody cared to nurse it, and that morning, as the women came in to the market, they still heard its feeble cries. Mary flew to the spot and found the baby, alive indeed but almost eaten up by the flies and insects that swarmed over it. Under her care it recovered and proved a singularly sweet and pretty little girl. Mary gave the child her own name and lived to see her happily married to David, an educated native from Lagos, and the proud driver of a Government motor car.

Another great battle had to be fought against heathen funeral customs. Only a few months before Mary Slessor went to Okoyong the funeral of a petty chief was celebrated by the burial along with him of four free wives, sixteen slaves and twenty boys and girls. The death of every person of importance was signalised by drunkenness, bloodshed, and the poison ordeal. Often Mary Slessor, taking her own life in her hand, stood between the living and the dead. One day Mr. Ovens, the carpenter from Duke Town who had been sent up to repair her house, was working on the roof when he heard a wild cry from the forest. Mary was off in a moment, and following he found her beside the unconscious form of a young man. It was Etim, the eldest son of the chief Edem, lying crushed under a heavy log. For a fortnight Mary nursed him, but in vain.

"Sorcerers have killed my son, and they must die," exclaimed the chief fiercely. "Bring the witch doctor."

He came and, after some incantations, laid the guilt on a neighbouring village near the scene of the accident. Soon a dozen men and women were in chains awaiting execution. Meantime Mary had not been idle. To propitiate the people and maintain a grip of the situation she took charge of the funeral arrangements, and proceeded to carry them through, with thoroughgoing barbaric splendour. She arrayed the body in the finest clothes she could procure, while the head, after being shaved and painted yellow, was crowned with a tall hat adorned with gorgeous plumes. Thus attired the body was seated in an arm chair under an umbrella, with a whip and walking stick in both hands, and a mirror in front to delight the spirit of the dead man with the reflection of all his glory. The natives danced in ecstasy at the sight. But the danger was not yet past.

"This is going to be a serious business," said Mary to Mr. Ovens.

"We can't leave these prisoners for a moment. I'll watch beside them all night, and you'll take the day."

Then the weary vigil began. The chief had great respect for the white Ma, but he was determined to honour his son with blood. Mary pled the cause of the prisoners and one or two were released. She got Mr. Ovens to make a coffin for the dead boy, and two missionaries were hurried up from Creek Town with a magic lantern to honour the occasion still further. To uninstructed eyes it would all have seemed a bit of melodramatic farce, but in reality it was a grim struggle for human lives. And in the end she won. The last of the prisoners was released and only a cow was sacrificed at the grave. It was the first chief's grave in Okoyong that was not saturated with human blood.

Gradually her sway over the tribe increased till she became by common consent an arbiter in all sorts of disputes. Sometimes she would sit a whole day quietly knitting while she listened to the interminable speeches of the opposing parties, so that they might feel that they had been allowed to say their utmost before she gave her decision.

V: *Essential Justice*

In 1891 the British Government, which was at that time extending its authority into the interior, recognised her unique position and appointed her Vice-consul for Okoyong. It was a post for which she had no liking, but she accepted it in the belief that she could thereby help to tide her people over the difficult transition time that lies between savagery and civilised governments. In this she was singularly successful, and was able to report in 1894: "No tribe was formerly so feared because of their utter disregard of human life, but human life is now safe. No chief ever died without the sacrifice of many lives, but this custom has now ceased. Some chiefs, gathered for palaver at our house, in commenting on the wonderful change, said, 'Ma, you white people are God Almighty. No other power could have done this.' "

With the Government officials she was always on the best of terms, and one of them has given a lively description of her personal appearance and original methods of court work. "A little frail old lady with a lace shawl over her head and shoulders (that must, I think, have been a concession to a stranger, for I never saw the thing again), swaying herself in a rocking chair and crooning to a black baby in her arms. I remember being struck—most unreasonably—by her very strong Scotch accent. Her welcome was everything kind and cordial. I had had a long march, it was an appallingly hot day, and she insisted on complete rest before we proceeded to the business of the court. It was held just below her house. Her compound was full of litigants, witnesses, and onlookers, and it was impressive to see how deep was the respect with which she was treated by them all. She was again in her rocking chair, surrounded by several ladies and babies-in-waiting, nursing another infant.

"I have had a good deal of experience of Nigerian courts of various kinds, but have never met one which better deserves to be termed a Court of Justice than that over which she presided. The litigants emphatically got justice—sometimes, perhaps, like Shylock, "more than they desired"—and it was essential justice, unhampered by legal technicalities. One decision I recall—I have often wished that I could follow it as a precedent. A sued B for a small debt. B admitted owing the money, and the Court (that is Ma) ordered him to pay accordingly. But she added, 'A is a rascal. He treats his mother shamefully, he neglects his children; only the other day he beat one of his wives, yes and she was B's sister too; his farm is a disgrace, he seldom washes, and then there was the palaver about C's goat a month ago. Oh, of course, A did not steal it, he was found not guilty, wasn't he?—all the same the affair was never satisfactorily cleared up, and he did look unusually sleek just about then. On the other hand B was thrifty and respectable. So, before B paid the amount due, he would give A a good, sound caning in the presence of everybody.' "

VI: *The Church of Christ in Okoyong*

Amid these varied labours and struggles she never ceased to plead with loving insistence the claims of Christ. She conducted service, taught the children in school, and visited the people in their homes. She was no organiser, as she herself well knew. Indeed, so absorbed in mind was she and so irregular in habits, that not infrequently she lost count of the days of the week, and would be found mending the roof of the house on Sunday and holding Church service on Monday. But one thing never failed, her spirit of passionate devotion and unwearying love.

In 1896, under the compulsion of ill health and yielding to the urgency of the Committee, she came to Scotland on furlough, bringing with her no fewer than four of her black children. Their presence excited much interest throughout the Church, but Mary herself, who could face a mob of savages, proved to be the most timid of missionary speakers, and absolutely refused to proceed if a man appeared in the audience. Even the inevitable chairman was only tolerated if he kept out of sight. Children, however, white as well as black, were her unfailing delight and she made troops of little friends everywhere. Speaking of Okoyong she expressed her feeling that her work there was done. The time, she said, had come for a Church to be organised in the district, and for her to move farther on into the interior. It was three years before this desire was gratified.

Returning to Calabar she resumed her work in Okoyong. Her last years there were saddened by the loss of many of her old friends through an epidemic of smallpox. She had removed from Ekenge to a more populous centre at Akpap, and she turned her old house into a hospital. Many of the people fled and left her to fight the disease single-handed. Her own chief, Edem, caught the infection and she nursed him till he died. With her own hands she made his coffin, dug his grave, and buried him. Next day two missionaries arrived from Creek Town and found her completely prostrate. When they visited her house at Ekenge they found it full of corpses, and not a living soul near.

The epidemic passed and her work resumed its normal course. At last she had the joy of seeing a little church organised, and of sitting at the Lord's Table with a company of those whom she had led out of heathen darkness into the Christian light.

VII: *The Pioneer of the Enyong Creek*

Meantime big events were happening in Calabar. The country to the west of the Cross River had never been penetrated by the white man. Powerful cannibal tribes occupied the whole of the Ibo country right across to the Niger. Little was known of them save the ominous fact that they poured down the Enyong Creek a continuous stream of slaves to the great slave market at Itu. A renowned centre of their barbarous worship was at Arochuku, near the head of the Creek, where stood a famous idol known as the Long Ju-Ju. Pilgrims to this shrine were often seized and offered in sacrifice or sold as slaves. In 1902 a British force marched to Arochuku, subdued the tribes, and demolished the Ju-Ju. Thus a vast and densely populated country was thrown open to the Gospel.

Mary Slessor felt an irresistible call to go in and possess the land. "I feel drawn on and on," she said, "by the magnetism of this land of dense darkness and mysterious weird forest." The Mission Council, recognising her exceptional gifts, gave her a roving commission to pioneer along the line of the Enyong Creek. At the age of fifty-four she set out on this new adventure, with the same fervour of spirit as she had entered Okoyong, and she was spared for twelve years more of toil and achievement. She established herself first at Itu, the old slave market at the mouth of the Creek, and later, when a medical missionary was settled there, she pushed on up country. Now that the power of the Ju-Ju had been broken the people everywhere were crying out for teachers, not from any pure thirst for the Gospel but to learn if possible the secret of the white man's power. It was impossible to meet the demand, and Mary could only travel incessantly along the Creek, building rest-huts for herself here and there, and endeavouring in this way to keep in touch with the seekers after light. Some of her own boys and girls from Okoyong gave assistance as teachers. The progress made was remarkable and included some of the most romantic episodes in her career.

On one of her earliest voyages down the Creek, a canoe shot out from the bank and she was invited to go ashore at a place called Akani Obio. Here she was taken to the house of a chief, Onoyom by name, who told her a touching story of his career. As a boy he had once seen a Calabar missionary, and afterwards he had heard something of the Christian religion from an ex-teacher of the mission who had fallen into sin and drunkenness. Now he was eager to build a church for his people. In due time the church was built at a cost of £300, provided by Onoyom himself, and every Sunday morning the Union Jack was hoisted to intimate to all passers by upon the Creek that no trading was to be done that day. When, by and by, the chief and his wife were baptised, and Mary sat with them and other converts at the Lord's Table, it was to her "a foretaste of heaven." "Akani Obio," she said, "is now linked on to Calvary. I am sure our Lord will never keep it from my mother."

Her remarkable influence over the natives was again recognised by the Government, and in 1905 she was asked to become President of the native court for the district around Itu. She consented to undertake the work but refused the salary, which accordingly was paid into the Mission funds. She ably discharged the duties of her office till 1909, when she was compelled by failing strength to resign the post. She continued, however, to preserve the happiest relations with the young Government officials, who treated their Ma with a teasing affection that masked a deep respect. She was by common consent the mother of the country, and her fame had travelled all along the West Coast. Her vitality and youthfulness of spirit were a continual marvel. Receiving a goat in a present at a certain village she led it home through the forest gaily singing, "Mary had a little lamb." She might seem eccentric and a bit of a character, but no one who knew her could fail to be impressed by her devotion and strong sense.

One of her Government friends having presented her with a bicycle she learned to ride, and while laughing at herself as a silly old woman on a wheel, she rejoiced in the help it gave her in her work. Soon, however, she was forbidden to cycle, and in her last years she was pushed along in a kind of a light rickshaw when too feeble to walk. Much of her work was done by canoe, and when she was asked how she was able to endure the long voyages on the Creek, she confessed that she took as big a dose of laudanum as she dared, and tried to sleep it out.

VIII: *The Happiest Woman in All the World*

In 1912 her health seemed completely shattered, and her friends arranged for a short holiday in the Canary Islands. She consented in the hope that it might restore her strength for another year or two of service. It was the one perfect holiday of her life, and the story of it reads like an idyll. Everybody conspired to surround her with love and care. She was a child in money matters, and her little cash box was passed on from Duke Town to the boat, from the boat to the hotel, and back again to Duke Town without suffering any diminution in its contents. She on her part made friends everywhere. A frail little old lady, with a face wrinkled like yellow parchment, she endeared herself to all by her simplicity and sympathy and love of fun. "What love is wrapped round me," she wrote. "It is simply wonderful. I can't say anything else. . . . Oh, if I only get another day to work. I hope it will be more full of earnestness and blessing than the past."

Shortly after her return to Calabar she received from the King the silver cross of the Order of St. John of Jerusalem, an honour, as the official letter stated, "only conferred on persons professing the Christian faith who are eminently distinguished for philanthropy." The presentation was made at Duke Town, and Mary was glad to escape back to the Creek, declaring she could "never face the world again after all this blarney."

Her mind was ever busy with new projects. She founded an industrial home for women and girls near Itu. She sent urgent appeals home for new workers. She pressed the advantage of using motor cars to increase the mobility of the missionaries. If they were profitable for Government work, she argued, why not for Christ's work? For herself, she kept moving incessantly from place to place until at last she persuaded every town of any consequence in the district to receive a Christian teacher. On the surrender of Ibam, the last town to hold out, she sat down on the floor of her hut, and leaning her back against the mud wall, she wrote to her friends in Scotland that she was "the happiest and most grateful woman in all the world."

Her long day of service was almost done. The last blow was the war. The news reached her at Odore Ikpe, her farthest outstation, five miles beyond the head of the Creek, where she was building a house. After reading of the invasion of Belgium and the retreat from Mons she tried to rise from her seat but found she had lost the power. Her native girls put her to bed where she lapsed into unconsciousness and seemed on the point of death. Thoroughly alarmed the girls had her carried the five miles to the Creek and put into a canoe which took her down to Itu. Here she lay on the ground at the landing place till the doctor came down and had her carried to her house. Under his care she rallied for a time. But the war was ever in her thoughts like a nightmare. "Oh, if I were thirty years younger," she cried, "and if I were a man!" She persisted in returning to her work, though when conducting service in the little church she had to remain seated and to lean hard on the communion table. This she continued to do by sheer force of will even to the last Sunday of her life.

She died on Wednesday, the 13th of January, 1915, just as the dawn was breaking. Her body was taken down the river by loving hands and buried in the cemetery on Mission Hill at Duke Town. As the procession approached the grave amid the wailing of the people, an aged native woman struck the right note.

"*Kutua oh, kutua oh,*" she exclaimed. "Do not cry, do not cry. Praise God from whom all blessings flow. Ma was a great blessing." It was a simple but perfect eulogy. Mary Slessor was indeed a great blessing. She gave to heathen Africa a new conception of womanhood, and to the world at large an imperishable example of Christian devotion.

THE END